GUARDING LOVE

THE DIVORCE-PROOFING AMERICA'S MARRIAGES
CAMPAIGN PRESENTS:

GUARDING LOVE

BY DR. GARY AND BARBARA ROSBERG

Tyndale House Publishers, Inc.
Wheaton, Illinois

Visit Tyndale's exciting Web site at www.tyndale.com

Guarding Love

Copyright © 2003 by Gary and Barbara Rosberg. All rights reserved.

Cover photograph copyright © 2003 by Brian MacDonald. All rights reserved.

Authors' photo copyright © 2002 by Thomas and Bruce Photography. All rights reserved.

Interior illustrations copyright © 2002 by Mona Caron. All rights reserved.

Designed by Julie Chen

Edited by Linda K. Taylor

Produced with the assistance of The Livingstone Corporation (www.LivingstoneCorp.com).

Published in association with the literary agency of Alive Communications, Inc., 7680 Goddard Street, Suite 200, Colorado Springs, CO 80920.

Unless otherwise indicated, all Scripture quotations are taken from the *Holy Bible*, New Living Translation, copyright © 1996. Used by permission of Tyndale House Publishers, Inc., Wheaton, Illinois 60189. All rights reserved.

All quotations are taken from *Guard Your Heart* by Dr. Gary and Barbara Rosberg, published by Tyndale House, 2002.

ISBN 0-8423-7344-6

Printed in the United States of America.

09 08 07 06 05 04 03

7 6 5 4 3 2 1

Dedication

To our ministry team at America's Family Coaches,
Thank you for serving so well.

To the Board of America's Family Coaches,
Thank you for leading us and helping us keep our focus.

To the men of CrossTrainers.
Thank you for being the best men in America.

To our America's Family Coaches...*Live!* listeners,
Thank you for allowing us to minister to you daily on radio.

To you, our readers,
Thank you for allowing us to partner with you in building divorced proofed marriages.

To Linda Taylor and Team Tyndale,
Our deepest thanks. Without you, this project would never be completed.

And most of all, to our family,
We love you!

CONTENTS

A SPECIAL NOTE FROM GARY AND BARB

Dear friends,

We are so glad that you have decided to spend several weeks on learning more about your spouse's needs and how to meet them. We know that your time will reap significant benefits—not only in your own marriage but also in the people on whom your marriage has an impact: your children, your larger family, your friends, your community, and beyond. You may be surprised by that list, but we really believe that the health of our marriages affects lots of people.

When you decided to do this workbook, you became part of a large group of couples across this nation—from Boston to Los Angeles, from Miami to Seattle—who are joining together to divorce-proof their marriages. They are taking a stand *for* healthy, growing, lifetime marriages and *against* the looming threat of divorce.

Most of you will be working through this book in the context of a small group; that's the most effective environment because you benefit from each other's perspectives, encouragement, prayer, and accountability. But even if you are going through the book on your own, we know you and your marriage will be changed.

This book is part of our larger campaign, Divorce-Proofing America's Marriages. The flagship book in that campaign, *Divorce-Proof Your Marriage,* outlines six loves—forgiving love, serving love, persevering love, guarding love, celebrating love, and renewing love—that will strengthen your marriage and keep you from sliding toward disappointment, discord, and possibly even emotional divorce.

This workbook is a companion to *Guard Your Heart,* which addresses the component of guarding love. If you haven't read *Divorce-Proof Your Marriage* and worked through the companion workbook, *Discover the Love of Your Life All Over Again,* that's all right. But your group may want to do that sometime in the future. (For a list of other campaign products, see the appendix at the back of this book, or log on to our Web site at **www.divorceproof.com.**)

We wish you God's richest blessings as you learn to serve your spouse by learning how to guard your heart.

Your friends,
Gary and Barb Rosberg

Introduction

HOW TO USE THIS BOOK

This workbook and its companion book, *Guard Your Heart,* by Gary and Barbara Rosberg are part of a series of studies based on a national campaign called Divorce-Proofing America's Marriages.

Based on their years of ministry and counseling to thousands of couples, the Rosbergs believe that Christian marriages are more threatened today than ever before. That is why they have joined forces with Christian leaders from around the country to give Christian couples the motivation and the tools to stand strong in the face of all threats to a pure and vibrant marriage.

Contained in this eight-session workbook study are biblical principles that will protect and quite possibly save your marriage. Even if you are one of many Christian couples who would never consider divorce, the emotional and spiritual intimacy of your marriage can deepen in ways you never thought possible. The principles are of no value to you if you do not use them, however. That is why we have developed the workbook study.

This is not a lecture that you simply attend. This is a workbook study that you and your spouse interact with together. The key to its significance in your marriage is in your hands. If you take advantage of what this course has to offer, your relationship will never be the same. You will discover things about yourself and your spouse that our enemy, Satan, doesn't want you to know because he realizes that a great Christian marriage is powerful.

In order to receive all that this workbook study has to offer, we ask that you commit to do the following:

- *Read the book.* Our book, *Guard Your Heart,* will draw you and your spouse together as you realize God's best intentions for your marriage.
- *Attend the group sessions.* There is much to gain from the insights of others.
- *Do your weekly homework assignments.* If you fail here, you will lose most of what this course has to offer you and your spouse.
- *Be aware of the spiritual battles that are yet to come.* That's right, *yet to come.* Once you begin to implement the principles of guarding love, Satan will go on the offensive against you. We do not have to fear him, but we do have to acknowledge his activities. However, the power of this course is the Person behind the principles, our Savior Jesus Christ. And he has already achieved the victory against our enemy.

Each week you will meet with your group for some general discussion (don't worry, no baring of your soul or pouring out your heart in front of others). The group discussion is to guide you to think about the topic. Included in the group time is a time for just you and your spouse to talk as well.

The heart of the study, however, comes in the homework assignments. After each group lesson you will find three sections for you to work on during the week. The topic you and your spouse discuss during the week will be highlighted further in the next group discussion time. So your preparation will not only be a time of reflection for you and your spouse but will give you direction for the next group session.

- **Day One** is a time of **Personal Reflection**. You will be asked some personal questions to consider as you think about the various topics discussed in the book.
- **Day Two** is a time for **Couple Interaction**. Here you and your spouse will talk together about your answers to the Personal Reflection time as well as about some other questions.
- **Day Three** is called **My Assignment**. This is a place to journal your thoughts about your progress. Don't worry—no one else will read this!

You are embarking on a marital journey that may very well change the way you love your spouse. Ask God to empower you to be a need-meeting husband or wife. This will be an exciting journey for both of you, as you discover how to

Guard Your Heart!

Group Session One

CHRISTIAN MARRIAGES UNDER ATTACK

Think of your marriage as a beautiful medieval castle. You have built it to perfection. It stands tall and imposing, overseeing its domain. It is a place of refuge and protection. It is strong and awesome in appearance. It has high turrets where watchmen can see for miles around, able to warn the inhabitants of impending danger in plenty of time to fortify the battlements and defeat any foe. It has high walls to repel any danger. It has a moat to keep intruders far away from the walls. It has a strong drawbridge—built of thick timbers, attached by heavy chains, and manned by fearsome guards. When the drawbridge comes up, nothing goes in or out. The castle is safe.

Now think of the medieval castles that dot the landscape of Europe today. For most of them, the glory is long gone. The walls have tumbled, the gate has fallen, the moat is dry. Sometime in the past, an enemy breached the walls and destroyed the castle. Or perhaps its inhabitants just didn't take care of it and allowed the wooden drawbridge to rot or the walls to crumble.

How's your "marriage castle"? Are the walls experiencing some cracks? Are the watchmen no longer in the turrets?

Let's do some castle remodeling and reinforcing. Let's look around and fix what needs to be repaired. Let's strengthen our castle, for the enemy is on his way to do battle.

OPEN THE DRAWBRIDGE

You should have already read part 1 of *Guard Your Heart*, chapters 1 and 2. Chapter 1 discusses the undeniable fact that the enemy, Satan, seeks to storm your marriage castle, tear it down, and bring it to ruin. Chapter 2 explains what it means for you to guard your heart and why such guarding love is vital in order to protect your marriage. This chapter also introduces six common areas of attack by Satan on marriages.

Why are so many Christian marriages hurting or in jeopardy of getting a divorce? Research indicates that Christians are divorcing at nearly the same rate as non-Christians. List below what you believe are some of the major threats to Christian marriages today.

What is a *threat*? A threat is anything that tempts a person to do something that would hurt his or her marriage. The threat, in and of itself, may not be a sin (such as, a person's career). However, a threat can tempt a person to sin if he or she is not careful. For example, a person could spend so much time focusing on a career that his or her spouse is neglected.

1. As a group, list at least five common threats to Christian marriages:

    _____

    _____

    _____

2. Why would each of these be considered a threat to a marriage? What can allow these threats to destroy a marriage? List as many ways as you can think of below:

    _____

    _____

    _____

STAND GUARD

As a group, read the following verses, and answer the questions:

> Above all else, guard your heart, for it affects everything you do.
> (Proverbs 4:23)

> The human heart is most deceitful and desperately wicked. Who really knows how bad it is? But I know! I, the Lord, search all hearts and examine secret motives. I give all people their due rewards, according to what their actions deserve. (Jeremiah 17:9-10)

> God blesses those whose hearts are pure, for they will see God.
> (Matthew 5:8)

> Jesus replied, "The most important commandment is this: 'Hear, O Israel! The Lord our God is the one and only Lord. And you must love the Lord your God with all your heart, all your soul, all your mind, and all your strength.'" (Mark 12:29-30)

3. Based on these verses, as a group complete the statements below:

- My heart affects _____ that I do.
- I really don't know how _____ my heart can get.
- God examines my _____.
- If my heart is _____, I will understand God better.
- The most important thing that God wants me to do is to love him with _____ of my _____.

4. Now, as a group, answer the following multiple choice statements, and consider the implications of the verses we just read. Check any that apply.

When it comes to certain sins, people should understand that they are . . .
☐ not capable of committing such sins so they need not worry about them.
☐ vulnerable to any sin, but if they are guarding their hearts, they can avoid them.
☐ not able to resist some sins because they are overwhelming.

When it comes to guarding their hearts, believers should be . . .
☐ mature enough Christians that they don't worry about it.
☐ immune to certain sins.
☐ always vigilant and regularly examining their hearts to protect themselves and their marriages.

If a marriage is not as good as a person would like it to be, the first thing he or she should do is . . .
☐ get counseling for the spouse.
☐ read more books.
☐ listen to more Christian music.
☐ examine his or her own heart, and be honest with God about what is going on.

A pure-hearted person is one whose . . .
☐ motives are unmixed.
☐ thoughts are always holy.
☐ conscience is clean.
☐ desire is to have his or her own needs met first.
☐ love is conditional.

5. God warns us to be careful because our hearts are _____.

Gary and Barb say:

The warnings of Scripture are very relevant to our marriages and families. You and your spouse, along with your children, are near the top of the enemy's hit list. Your marriage is God's creation; your family is God's joy. So Satan is working hard to destroy your family relationship, demoralize you, and discredit your witness. He wants to isolate you from each other, from the Lord, and from other Christian families.

That's why we need the Lord—as individuals, couples, and families. That's why we need each other as husbands and wives. And that's why we need other believers around us: fellow church members, a Bible study group, a home fellowship group, or an accountability group. As a spouse and parent, you need someone to watch your back, monitor your blind spots, and walk beside you over the long haul. It's nearly impossible to guard your heart, your marriage, and your family alone. . . .

Behind every attack on your marriage and family is the master terrorist, Satan. Whatever strategy he may use to come after you, he always goes for the heart. That's why we need to guard our hearts. Because just when we begin to relax our guard, thinking our marriage is invulnerable to attack, he swoops in and nails us. As you will see shortly, if the enemy can get to your heart and the heart of your marriage, he has a good chance of bringing you down.

(pages 7–8)

ON THE WATCHTOWER

For this section, you and your spouse need to work together in a semiprivate spot in the room to answer the following questions:

6. Are you being as careful as you should be when it comes to protecting your marriage? Each of you individually should complete the statements below by circling the number for each statement that best describes how you feel about your marriage (1 = do not agree; 5 = strongly agree). Then share your answers, and record your spouse's responses in the empty chart below your own.

How I Feel about Our Marriage

I am doing everything I can to protect my marriage.

<u>1   2   3   4   5</u>

Our marriage has been through some tough times, but we are stronger for them.

<u>1   2   3   4   5</u>

My spouse and I are doing everything we can to protect each other.

1   2   3   4   5

I demonstrate to my spouse that he or she is the most important person in my life.

1   2   3   4   5

Our children would say that we have a great marriage. (If you don't have children, what would your friends say?)

1   2   3   4   5

How My Spouse Feels about Our Marriage
Circle the number your spouse selected.

I am doing everything I can to protect my marriage.

1   2   3   4   5

Our marriage has been through some tough times, but we are stronger for them.

1   2   3   4   5

My spouse and I are doing everything we can to protect each other.

1   2   3   4   5

I demonstrate to my spouse that he or she is the most important person in my life.

1   2   3   4   5

Our children would say that we have a great marriage. (If you don't have children, what would your friends say?)

1   2   3   4   5

PREPARE FOR THE WEEK

As Gary and Barb have noted, marriages are under attack. In this study, you will focus on six key areas of attack. As any good soldier will tell you, knowing what the enemy is up to is vital information. It is the surprise attacks that are the most deadly (remember Pearl Harbor and 9/11). We know what our enemy, Satan, is up to. He wants nothing more than to see your nice Christian marriage become cool and indifferent, if not a complete battleground that ends in divorce. While his attacks will be slightly different for different couples, we still know that he will focus on at least one of six areas:

Career and home pressures
The allure of status and stuff
Relationship pressures
Sexual temptation
Misguided views of success
Passivity and control

We will look at facets of these over the next few weeks. Don't be tempted to think that you are immune to any one of these concerns (remember the verses you just studied?). As we consider these areas of concentration by our enemy, we will also discuss how to guard our own heart and our spouse's heart. In this way, we will reinforce our castle walls and be ready and able to fight back when he attacks.

As a group, discuss the following five ground rules one by one.

1. CONCENTRATE ON YOUR SPOUSE'S NEEDS
Take the responsibility to "give" to your spouse and trust that God will meet your own needs however he chooses. By being "other focused" and concerned about meeting your spouse's needs first, you may be surprised how God will bless you by involving your mate in meeting each of your own needs.

2. AVOID CRITICISM
When it comes time for your spouse to focus on your needs, be careful not to be critical of how he or she hasn't met your past needs. Never criticize your mate to the group.

3. KEEP YOUR GROUP SHARING TIME SAFE
Some, if not all, in your group will want to share the progress that each is making from week to week. Keep your sharing time confidential within your group, and avoid comparing each other's marriage relationships. Make your group a safe place to share your strengths and struggles.

4. FOCUS ON "BEING" AS WELL AS "DOING"
Meeting our spouse's needs involves "doing" something. But our "doing" is empow-

ered by our "being" something. As our attitudes are transformed, our behavior changes. So throughout this course you will be asked to focus on certain Christ-like attitudes that will direct your actions.

5. COMPLETE YOUR WEEKLY EXERCISES AND ASSIGNMENTS

You will be asked to spend a couple of hours each week between these group sessions in discovering how to better meet your spouse's needs.

This week you will need to read chapter 3 of Guard Your Heart.

Plan and practice how you will guard your heart against the pressure that comes when your career and home are out of balance. You will do this in part by completing your Personal Reflection Time and by looking for opportunities to demonstrate to your spouse that you are not going to allow the pressures of life to damage your relationship.

Schedule your Couple's Interaction time. Get it on your calendar before you go to bed tonight.

Journal your progress by writing down what you did to practice meeting your spouse's need and chronicle his or her response.

Week One—Day One
MY PERSONAL REFLECTION:
KEEPING LIFE BALANCED

During the week, you and your spouse should read chapter 3 in *Guard Your Heart*. Chapter 3 focuses on job and home pressures.

Are the pressures of life damaging your marriage? Would your spouse say that you are giving him or her the best you have to offer? How about your children? These questions are difficult to wrestle with because it is difficult to keep life balanced.

During this time of reflection you will be asked to be honest with yourself. You will compare the time, energy, and attention you invest in your career or home with the time, energy, and attention you invest in your spouse.

Most of us have primary responsibilities in at least one of these two areas. Perhaps you have both a career *and* you assume most of the responsibilities for taking care of your home. If this is the case, you and your spouse need to talk about the excessive demands this places on you. For now, choose one area (career or home) and take the following survey.

This survey is based on how I manage my (circle one): Career   Home

1. Are you taking care of your responsibilities in a way that is pleasing to the Lord? Explain.

    _____

    _____

    _____

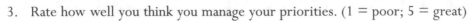

2. Rate your level of motivation for your responsibilities. (1 = "I want to quit"; 5 = "I am highly motivated")

    1 2 3 4 5

3. Rate how well you think you manage your priorities. (1 = poor; 5 = great)

    1 2 3 4 5

4. Rate your attitude toward your responsibilities. (1 = very bad 5 = very good)

    1 2 3 4 5

5. Is your spouse getting choice, generous, and consistent servings of your mental and emotional energy? Do you give your spouse *quantity* time as well as *quality* time? (1 = only what is left over; 5 = always the best I have)

    1 2 3 4 5

Conclude this Personal Reflection exercise by praying and writing a prayer that expresses the following:

> Lord, I thank you for my spouse because
>
> _____
>
> I pray for my marriage and ask that you will
>
> _____
>
> I pray for my spouse and ask you to bless him or her by
>
> _____
>
> Please help me to keep my life properly balanced. Show me what I need to change in my life to avoid neglecting my spouse's needs. Amen.

Week One—Day Two

COUPLE INTERACTION:
KEEPING LIFE BALANCED

You will need to set aside about thirty minutes to complete this exercise with your spouse. Be sure you have selected a place where you will not be interrupted (turn off the phones, pagers, and find a location that will allow you to comfortably share with each other).

Begin your time together in prayer. As each of you prays, focus on the following:

- that you will share with an attitude of love for your spouse and commitment to the process of making any adjustments necessary in your life to defeat the enemies of your heart.
- that you will avoid focusing on how your spouse has disappointed you. Rather, focus on what the two of you can do now to improve your relationship.
- that you will be open to what your spouse shares with you.
- that God will be glorified by your marriage.

1. Share with your spouse how you answered the survey questions from your Personal Reflection time. After you have shared your survey responses, ask your spouse to indicate how he or she would answer the survey questions about you. Listen to your spouse's responses without asking any questions or challenging the answers. Circle your spouse's answers to the survey in your workbook. If possible, use a different color pen or in some other way identify your spouse's answers on your survey.

2. Now, ask your spouse to explain why he or she gave you these particular ratings. After your spouse shares, voice your commitment to make any adjustments necessary to enable you to give the time, energy, and attention your spouse needs.

Conclude your time in prayer. Ask God to give each of you the courage to make changes in your life, as necessary. Make a commitment to regularly come together just to evaluate your marriage.

Week One—Day Three

MY ASSIGNMENT:
KEEPING LIFE BALANCED

You have two assignments this week:

1. Read chapter 3 of *Guard Your Heart*. Have you completed that assignment yet?

   ❏ Yes   ❏ No   ❏ I've started, but I have more to read.

2. Make one sacrifice for your spouse this week.

Your assignment is to rearrange your work schedule or give up some activity that you enjoy so you can spend some quality time with your spouse. The point is to give up something you would normally do (for example, go in to work later in the morning so you can have breakfast with your spouse; put off doing the laundry; do housework together; etc.). Make all necessary arrangements, including informing your spouse of what you intend to give up and when. Then, ask your spouse to decide what the two of you will do together. Make this a time focused solely on your spouse.

My Journal

How did your Couple Interaction time go? Were there any insights or breakthroughs? Explain.

_____

_____

_____

_____

_____

_____

_____

_____

_____

_____

Here is what I did to spend time with my spouse this week and what we did together.

_____

_____

_____

_____

_____

_____

_____

_____

_____

_____

Group Session Two

GUARDING THE BALANCE OF CAREER AND HOME

OPEN THE DRAWBRIDGE

During the week, you and your spouse should have read chapter 3 of *Guard Your Heart*. Ideally you also made time to work through the homework assignments.

As the session begins, couples should work together to answer the following questions:

1. Write down the ways you and your spouse keep track of your schedules.

   _____

   _____

   _____

2. Do you feel that the two of you have enough time alone together?

   _____

   _____

   _____

It's amazing what we have to do to keep our busy lives on track. Many people must keep track of not only their own schedules but also but those of their spouse and children as well. Sometimes the calendar is so full we feel that all we do is run from one activity to the next. How many times in the last month have you said, "We are just so busy"?

Do you and your spouse ever feel as if you're no more than "ships that pass in the night"? Do you constantly run on empty, trying to make it to all kinds of commitments, appointments, engagements?

While there is nothing wrong with activity—surely many of the activities that we do involve good things—we need to not allow the very pressure of our schedule to cause breakdowns in our marriage.

And judging from the lack of time we have on our schedules, time is priceless!

We all have the same twenty-four hours every day. What can we do keep pressures from infringing on the very pleasure that our families can bring us?

STAND GUARD

How do we know when our lives are out of balance? What are the symptoms when we are not guarding our hearts and protecting our marriages from the pressures of life? Several are mentioned below. Discuss as a group how the situations described below could cause problems in a marriage. Write your answers on the lines.

3. People's lives are out of balance when . . .

   They accept a job only to acquire more possessions.

   _____

   _____

   _____

   They are more fulfilled at work than they are in their marriage.

   _____

   _____

   _____

   They feel distant from their spouse because they don't spend time together.

   _____

   _____

   _____

   They are exhausted every evening and have no energy left for their spouse.

   _____

   _____

   _____

They can't remember the last time they attended their children's activities.

_____

_____

_____

They spend more time with their possessions than they do with their spouse.

_____

_____

_____

Other: _____

_____

_____

4. What do the following verses say about what God expects of us?

    > Work hard and cheerfully at whatever you do, as though you were working for the Lord rather than for people. (Colossians 3:23)

    God expects us to

    _____

    But those who won't care for their own relatives, especially those living in the same household, have denied what we believe. Such people are worse than unbelievers. (1 Timothy 5:8)

    God expects us to

    _____

    God commands us to work hard and cheerfully. He expects us to care for our family's needs. In our culture, we do that most often by going away to a job. The key, then, is to guard our hearts against allowing work and home responsibilities to get out of balance.

    Gary and Barb say:
    For most of us, work itself is not inherently dangerous. But any kind of work out of balance is dangerous to the health of your marriage and family. What is work out of balance? When you work provides for your family in some areas—such as meeting financial and

material needs—but robs your family in other areas—such as emotional, relational, and spiritual health—it is dangerously out of balance. . . .

Just as there are temptation and opportunities for careers to slip out of balance, women and men whose primary work is the care of home and children can find themselves dangerously unbalanced. . . . If you allow your daily schedule to be dictated solely by what should be done or could be done around the house, you wouldn't have any time for anything else. Such an unbalanced life leaves any number of important items unguarded and vulnerable to attack.
(pages 48, 53–54)

5. As a group, discuss some ways that either a husband's or wife's career can get out of balance and become a danger to unguarded hearts and an unguarded marriage.

_____

_____

_____

6. As a group, discuss ways that a husband's or wife's staying at home full time can cause a shift in balance and become a danger to a marriage.

_____

_____

_____

7. How can spouses balance working to provide and maintain a nice home with the need to keep a strong marriage and family life? What types of sacrifices may need to be made?

_____

_____

_____

ON THE WATCHTOWER

For this section, you and your spouse need to work together in a semiprivate spot in the room. First fill in the chart individually, then discuss each other's answers to the third column as noted in the instructions below.

8. On the chart below, record the five current activities that require the majority of your time, energy, and attention each week. This could be your job, home responsibilities, volunteer work, children's activities, etc.

My Top Five Activities	How much time does this activity take?	Is this the right amount of time or too much?
1. _____	_____	_____
2. _____	_____	_____
3. _____	_____	_____
4. _____	_____	_____
5. _____	_____	_____

Evaluate your activities with your spouse. Ask your spouse to review your list, and place a *?* next to each item that he or she feels takes too much of your time, energy, or attention.

If your spouse placed a *?* next to any of these activities, discuss what might be necessary in order to bring balance back to your life, back to your marriage, and back to your family.

You will have made huge strides in your marriage when you can look at and discuss this very important part of your daily lives. Sometimes the way we spend our time can be a contention—without our even knowing it. The husband may spend long hours at work thinking that this will please his wife because of the big paycheck he is earning; the wife may be angry that her husband is at work so much when she could do with less if he would just be at home more. So let's talk, clear the air, and guard our hearts against allowing the pressures we put on ourselves to become pressure points in our marriage.

PREPARE FOR THE WEEK

This week you will need to read chapter 4 of Guard Your Heart. *Closely tied with the pressure caused by having career and home out of balance is the pressure caused by a lack of contentment and materialism—the allure and accumulation of status and stuff.*

Plan to spend some time thinking honestly about your approach to your "stuff" and your desire for status.

Schedule your Couple's Interaction time. Get it on your calendar before you go to bed tonight.

Journal your progress by writing down what you did to practice meeting your spouse's need, and chronicle his or her response.

Week Two—Day One

MY PERSONAL REFLECTION: FINDING CONTENTMENT

During the week, you and your spouse should read chapter 4 in *Guard Your Heart*. Chapter 4 focuses on the trap of materialism.

How do you feel about your status in life? What about the stuff you have around you?

During this time of reflection you will again be asked to be honest with yourself. You need to seriously think about your level of contentment. Of course we all strive to better our lives, to reach new goals, to become all that God wants us to be, but sometimes our motives and goals get mixed up when our comparisons are not with what God wants but with what our neighbors have.

You will again take a survey to focus on these attitudes. Rate the answers from 1 to 5 (1 = never; 5 = a resounding yes).

1. Do you live for the weekend, good times, parties, fun? Would you rather be watching TV, playing golf, or going out with friends than anything else?

   1   2   3   4   5

2. Are you captivated by the next rung on the corporate ladder? Do you find yourself striving for authority or control in your relationships? Do you desire recognition above all else?

   1   2   3   4   5

3. Are you under the illusion that the next raise, the big sale, or winning the lottery will make your problems go away?

   1   2   3   4   5

4. Are you discontented with what you have, always yearning for a bigger home, newer car, nicer wardrobe, or the latest toys?

1   2   3   4   5

5. Is it vitally important to you to be known as chairperson, president, manager, leader, or some other title?

1   2   3   4   5

6. Do you feel that you have a balanced view of the status and stuff in your life? Does your pursuit of either of those take away from time with your spouse, time in your marriage? Explain.

_____

_____

_____

Conclude this Personal Reflection exercise by praying and writing a prayer that expresses the following:

Lord, I thank you for all that I have, including

_____

I confess that I am discontented about

_____

I ask you to give me a heart that is contented in this area. Show me in what areas of life I *should* be discontented because I need to let you teach me and change me; but also show me where I need to learn contentment so that I do not get distracted. Protect our marriage by giving us contentment. Amen.

Week Two—Day Two

COUPLE INTERACTION: FINDING CONTENTMENT

You will need to set aside about thirty minutes to complete this exercise with your spouse. Be sure you have selected a place where you will not be interrupted (turn off the phones, pagers, and find a location that will allow you to comfortably share with each other).

Begin your time together in prayer. As each of you prays, focus on the following:

- that God will convict you of areas where you are allured by status and stuff to the detriment of your marriage.
- that God will show you how to be thankful for all you have been given.
- that you will be open to what your spouse shares with you.
- that God will be glorified by your marriage.

1. Share with your spouse how you answered the survey questions from your Personal Reflection time. After you have shared your survey responses, ask your spouse to indicate how he or she would answer the survey questions about you. Listen to your spouse's responses without asking any questions or challenging the answers. Circle your spouse's answers to the survey in your workbook. If possible, use a different color pen or in some other way identify your spouse's answers on your survey.

2. Now, ask your spouse to explain why he or she gave you these particular ratings. Also discuss your answers to question 6. After your spouse shares, voice your commitment to make any adjustments necessary to enable you to be contented

with what God has given you and to learn not to be overly enamored by what others have.

Conclude your time in prayer. Ask God to give each of you the courage to be thankful, to learn contentment, and to make sacrifices as needed in the areas of accumulating status and stuff.

Week Two—Day Three

MY ASSIGNMENT:
FINDING CONTENTMENT

You have two assignments this week:

1. Read chapter 4 of *Guard Your Heart*. Have you completed that assignment yet?

    ❑ Yes   ❑ No   ❑ I've started, but I have more to read.

2. Walk through your home this week and thank God for everything you see.

My Journal

How did your Couple Interaction time go? Were there any insights or breakthroughs? Explain.

_____

_____

_____

_____

_____

_____

_____

_____

_____

Here is what I did to make a difference in my attitude toward status and stuff.

_____

_____

_____

_____

_____

_____

_____

_____

_____

Group Session Three

GUARDING AGAINST MATERIALISM

OPEN THE DRAWBRIDGE

During the week, you and your spouse should have read chapter 4 of *Guard Your Heart*. Ideally you also made time to work through the homework assignments.

As the session begins, couples should work together to answer the following questions.

1. Do you think that you both have a habit of being thankful for all that you have? How do you show it?

    _____

    _____

    _____

2. Are there some areas in your life where you consistently feel like you need to "keep up with the Joneses"? Why do you think you feel that way?

    _____

    _____

    _____

In Group Session One we talked about the problem that occurs when our career and home get out of balance—when we place undue emphasis on our schedules and then forget to schedule time for our marriage!

The situation we will consider today is tied closely to that lack of balance. Often our schedules are overwhelmed because we are chasing after status and stuff. The motive behind those busy schedules is less than pristine. Perhaps we are driven by the need to work eighty hours a week in order to get that promotion or earn more money so we can buy more stuff so we can keep up with the neighbors who just got some new stuff. Perhaps we are deceiving ourselves into thinking that we're doing all this for our family—so they can have more stuff. Too often, however, we are doing all that when our marriages—and our families—need the most valuable thing we have: our time.

STAND GUARD

You've heard it before, but we'll say it again: there is a big difference between *needs* and *wants*. Below, on the left, is a list of needs. In the column on the right, list something that might be simply a *want* in that same category (the first one is suggested as an example).

Needs	**Wants**
Transportation	Have to have a top-of-the-line vehicle, even if too expensive for our budget
Job	
Housing	
Food	
Clothing	
Money	

3. In order to guard our hearts against the pressures of life, how would it help to clarify the difference between our *needs* and our *wants*? How can we know the difference?

   _____

   _____

4. Too often, marriage and family get neglected for one or more of the four P's: Beneath each word, describe how it could be a healthy desire as well as how it could become an unhealthy focus in a person's life.

Pleasure

_____

_____

_____

Power

_____

_____

_____

Possessions

_____

_____

_____

Position

_____

_____

_____

Read the following verses, and answer the questions.

> Yet true religion with contentment is great wealth. After all, we didn't bring anything with us when we came into the world, and we certainly cannot carry anything with us when we die. So if we have enough food and clothing, let us be content. (1 Timothy 6:6-8)

5. What does this say about our drives for the four P's in life?

_____

_____

_____

> For the love of money is at the root of all kinds of evil. And some people, craving money, have wandered from the faith and pierced themselves with many sorrows. (1 Timothy 6:10)

6. Is it wrong to earn money—even a lot of money? What does this verse mean?

_____

_____

_____

> Tell those who are rich in this world not to be proud and not to trust in their money, which will soon be gone. But their trust should be in the living God, who richly gives us all we need for our enjoyment.
> (1 Timothy 6:17)

7. How is it true that wealth is relative? You may not feel rich, but to someone else, you may be. How should you view your wealth, no matter how much you have?

_____

_____

_____

> Stay away from the love of money; be satisfied with what you have. For God has said, "I will never fail you. I will never forsake you."
> (Hebrews 13:5)

8. Is it okay to strive for more—to seek a better job, to earn more pay, to seek to better your position? How do you maintain a healthy balance?

_____

_____

_____

9. How would you describe a healthy attitude toward the four P's? Check all that apply.

❑ I can be satisfied with what I have, without the need for more.
❑ I am not afraid of losing my status or possessions.
❑ My security rests in my accomplishments.
❑ Sometimes I have to sacrifice what I want to give my spouse what he or she needs.
❑ My security rests in God alone.
❑ My needs are whatever God says they are; my wants are everything else.
❑ My priorities are driven by what God says is important.

Gary and Barb say:

[We] have noticed a more subtle home-disrupting distraction. . . . It's the comparison trap. Here the emphasis is not so much on what you have, what you do, or how much influence you wield. Rather, it's on how favorably your status and stuff compares with that of others. You may feel driven to make sure you measure up to—or exceed—the standards of the people you want to impress. . . . Don't put that kind of pressure on yourself or your spouse. It's no crime to wish and plan for nicer things and better conditions. But instead of living in dissatisfaction and disappointment, learn to say with the apostle Paul, "I have learned how to get along happily whether I have much or little. I know how to live on almost nothing or with everything. I have learned the secret of living in every situation, whether it is with a full stomach or empty, with plenty or little" (Philippians 4:11-12).
(pages 70–71)

ON THE WATCHTOWER

For this section, you and your spouse need to work together in a semiprivate spot in the room to answer the following questions.

10. Review the verses from Philippians in Gary and Barb's quote above. Do you think that you have learned as a couple to get along happily with much or little? Why or why not?

_____

_____

_____

11. Do you think you have learned the secret of contentment? What might you need to do in order to emulate the apostle Paul's attitude? Explain your answer.

_____

_____

_____

PREPARE FOR THE WEEK

This week you will read chapter 5 of Guard Your Heart. *The next couple of chapters discuss relational issues—how relationships can undermine our marriages if we don't guard our hearts.*

All of our relationships outside of the relationship with our spouse are very important. We need our friendships outside of our marriages. However, as you will discover when you read the next couple of chapters (or perhaps you've already discovered in your own life), if you do not guard your heart, you will find those relationships undermining your marriage.

Plan to spend some time thinking honestly about your outside relationships. Some may need to be cut loose. Others may need to have boundaries placed around them in order to keep them from becoming unhealthy.

Schedule your Couple Interaction time with your spouse.

Journal your progress in the pages provided.

Week Three—Day One

MY PERSONAL REFLECTION: SHOWING PARTIALITY TO MY SPOUSE

During the week, you and your spouse should read chapter 5 in *Guard Your Heart*. Chapter 5 discusses people/relational pressures.

There's no way around it—you're going to have people pressures in your life. Whether it be with your children, other relatives, friends, coworkers, bosses, employees, or people in your neighborhood, you're bound to run into downright frustrating situations. Through it all, however, you must always have your radar tuned to the frequency of the main relationship in your life (besides your relationship with God, of course): your relationship with your spouse.

Are you partial toward your spouse? Are you biased toward your marriage relationship? One definition for the word *bias* is "foregone conclusion." When it comes to your spouse, is it a foregone conclusion with you that he or she usually gets the best of your attention, affection, care, and concern? Obviously, every marriage has periods in which our responsibilities require more of our attention. The issue is that over time, we give our best to our marriage.

To help both of you evaluate your relationship, we are going to define four emotional needs that will be our focus this week. There are obviously many needs that we are to meet in our marriage relationship, but these four seem to be good indicators of the health of a marriage. These indicators are:

Attention—Regularly spending quality time with my spouse, giving him or her my undistracted attention.

Affection—Connecting with my spouse in a nonsexual manner that he or she has requested, without seeking anything in return.

Care—Taking the initiative to do things that will make my spouse's life more joyful, without having to be asked.

Concern—Thinking about my spouse throughout the day and praying for his or her needs.

1. Are you giving your best to your marriage? Give an example of a time when your spouse showed you attention, affection, care, and concern. Then explain how it made you feel when your spouse did that for you.

A time when my spouse showed me *attention:*

_____

_____

_____

When my spouse gives me *attention*, it makes me feel:

_____

_____

_____

A time when my spouse showed me *affection:*

_____

_____

_____

When my spouse shows me *affection*, I feel:

_____

_____

_____

A time when my spouse showed *care* for me:

_____

_____

_____

When my spouse *cares* for me, I feel:

_____

_____

_____

A time when my spouse showed *concern* for me:

_____

_____

_____

When my spouse shows *concern* for me, I feel:

_____

_____

_____

2. Conclude this Personal Reflection exercise in prayer. As you pray, focus on the following:

    ● Thank God for your spouse.
    ● Ask God to help you guard your heart against relationships that take away from your partiality toward your spouse.
    ● Ask forgiveness if you are giving your best to other people pressures and not to your marriage.
    ● Pray for specific needs your spouse has now.

Week Three—Day Two

COUPLE INTERACTION:
SHOWING PARTIALITY
TO MY SPOUSE

You will need to set aside about thirty minutes to complete this exercise with your spouse. Be sure you have selected a place where you will not be interrupted (turn off the phones, pagers, and find a location that will allow you to comfortably share with each other).

Begin your time together in prayer. As each of you prays, focus on the following:

- That you will share with an attitude of love for your spouse and a commitment to the process of making any adjustments necessary to defeat the enemies of your heart.
- That you will be able to be honest about the relational pressures facing your marriage.
- That you will be open to what your spouse shares with you.
- That God will be glorified by your marriage.

1. Share with your spouse how important he or she is to you. It is important to understand why your marriage relationship is so special and why it deserves your best. Tell your spouse how it makes you feel when he or she gives you attention, affection, care, and concern. Then ask your spouse to do the same thing, recording below what your spouse shares.

    When I give my spouse *attention*, it makes him or her feel:

    _____

    _____

When I show my spouse *affection*, he or she feels:

_____

_____

_____

When I show my spouse that I *care*, he or she feels:

_____

_____

_____

When I show my spouse *concern,* he or she feels:

_____

_____

_____

2. After you share, ask your spouse to answer how he or she thinks you are doing in giving your best when it comes to attention, affection, care, and concern.

Conclude your time in prayer. Ask God to give each of you the courage to make changes in your life, as necessary. Each of you read the following words to the other:

> (Your spouse's name), I want to affirm my devotion to you in the following ways:
>
> I vow to make myself accountable to you by giving you permission to ask me anything you want to know about my relationships. I will consider any concern you have if you believe that my relationships are hurting our marriage, even though I may disagree with you. And I will pray with you when we face people pressures that threaten our marriage.
>
> I also vow to love you genuinely and sincerely, and I will take the initiative to make sure you are not alone as you carry the burdens of your relationships. I promise to shoulder those burdens with you. I do all of this because I love you very much.

Week Three —Day Three

MY ASSIGNMENT:
SHOWING PARTIALITY TO MY SPOUSE

You have two assignments this week:

1. Read chapter 5 of *Guard Your Heart*. Have you completed that assignment yet?

    ❑ Yes   ❑ No   ❑ I've started, but I have more to read.

2. Focus on meeting one of the four emotional needs for your spouse this week (attention, affection, care, and concern). Select the one need that your spouse has indicated is the most lacking in your relationship, and make a special effort to meet that need this week.

My Journal

How did your Couple Interaction time go? Were there any insights or breakthroughs? Explain.

_____

_____

_____

_____

_____

_____

_____

_____

_____

_____

Here is what I did to show attention, affection, care, and/or concern to my spouse this week.

_____

_____

_____

_____

_____

_____

_____

_____

_____

Group Session Four

GUARDING AGAINST RELATIONAL PRESSURES

OPEN THE DRAWBRIDGE

During the week, you and your spouse should have read chapter 5 of *Guard Your Heart*. Ideally you also made time to work through the homework assignments.

As the session begins, couples should work together to answer the following questions:

1. Think of someone whom you believe is devoted 100 percent to his or her profession. This person could be an athlete, a national leader, a business leader, a church leader, etc. Write the person's name and his or her profession in the space below. Then, write one characteristic of this person that proves his or her devotion (one example is provided).

Name and Profession   **Characteristic that proves devotion**

Example: Tiger Woods—golfer   *On average, he plays golf 350 days every year.*

2. What kind of devotion do you think it takes to have a great marriage?

The pressures your marriage castle will face are numerous. People come and go from your life; situations in life change. No matter how impregnable your marriage fortress may feel today, if you don't keep it strong and secure, five years from now you could find yourself in a compromising situation. The kingdoms of old had to be careful about their alliances. An improper or unwise alliance could lead not only to defeat on the battlefield but to the end of the kingdom as well.

The relationships with the many people in our lives can cause stress or frustration that spills over into our marriage. Let's examine some of these situations today and explore what we can do to guard our hearts and our castles against improper relationships.

STAND GUARD

Consider the list of relationships that are on page 77 of *Guard Your Heart* and are listed below. Place a check mark next to any that you think could be making it difficult, if not impossible, to give your best to your spouse. Place the name of that person in the chart at question 3, and then write a brief explanation of why this relationship is having a negative effect on your marriage. The explanation may be that this relationship requires too much of your time (attention), or maybe it requires so much of your care and concern that your emotional energy is depleted and not available for your spouse.

- ❑ Your children—including stepchildren and your children's spouses
- ❑ Your grandchildren
- ❑ Your parents—including birth parents, stepparents, godparents
- ❑ Your spouse's parents
- ❑ Your siblings and their families
- ❑ Your grandparents
- ❑ Other extended family members—uncles, aunts, cousins, etc.
- ❑ Your circle of friends
- ❑ Your nearest neighbors
- ❑ Your superiors, peers, subordinates, and clients at work
- ❑ Committees, classes, or groups, at church
- ❑ Civic organizations, service clubs, or hobby groups, etc.
- ❑ Other: _____

3. The following relationships are making it difficult for me to give my best to my spouse:

The Relationship	The reason(s) it could be a problem
_____	_____
_____	_____
_____	_____

4. All of these are appropriate relationships, and you have some degree of responsibility to them. However, you need to be alert to warning signs that a relationship has become improper. As the leader gives you the answers, fill in the blanks below.

A legitimate relationship has become improper when . . .

I _____ my emotional, physical, and spiritual energy to the point that my _____ suffers.

I depend on this relationship to _____ _____ my spouse should meet.

I refuse to _____ to my spouse's concerns about this relationship.

I am not willing to ask my spouse for _____ with this relationship.

You may not have any one relationship that is overwhelming you, but all of your relationships taken together may add up to a life that is out of control. It is wise to periodically evaluate them with your spouse and make adjustments if you are so overburdened that you or your marriage is suffering.

How can you guard your heart against improper relationships? Consider the following three steps, filling in the blanks as a group, reading the verses, and answering the questions.

Three steps toward guarding your heart against relationship pressures

STEP #1: Be _____ to your spouse.

Submit to one another out of reverence for Christ. (Ephesians 5:21)

5. How can submitting to each other and being accountable to each other help spouses to guard their hearts?

_____

_____

_____

As fellow believers, we are expected to hold each other accountable for the way we live. This includes husbands and wives. Sometimes we are fearful of accountability because we misunderstand its application to marriage. For our purposes, we will apply accountability to marriage as the act of giving my spouse permission to be concerned about me and the welfare of our marriage. If we think about accountability in this way, we are in a better position to guard our heart against improper relationships.

STEP #2: Be _____ with your spouse.

> Don't just pretend that you love others. Really love them. Hate what is wrong. Stand on the side of the good. Love each other with genuine affection, and take delight in honoring each other. (Romans 12:9-10)

6. What does it mean to be "authentic" in a relationship? As a group, list some of the characteristics of an authentic person, and record these in the spaces below. This is a person who . . .

_____

_____

_____

If we are not authentic in our love and care for our spouse, our hearts are vulnerable to relationship pressures. God expects us to make a choice, even when we don't feel like it, to love our spouse with genuine affection.

STEP #3: Be _____ of your spouse.

> Don't think only about your own affairs, but be interested in others, too, and what they are doing. (Philippians 2:4)

7. What does it mean to be aware of one's spouse?

_____

_____

_____

8. How will these three steps help us to guard our hearts?

_____

_____

_____

Gary and Barb say:

This is a helpful way to look at the people problems in your life. Who is the most seriously wounded person in your circle of relationships today? Who genuinely needs you the most? Whose pain must be addressed to prevent more serious damage? . . . Maintain your priorities of meeting your own basic needs and the needs of your spouse. But keep an eye out for the needy others on the periphery, especially those who are in dangerous or painful situations. . . . People pressures will never go away in this lifetime. But you can guard your heart, guard your spouse, and guard your home against their harmful effects. As you exercise guarding love in your many relationships, beginning at home, you will notice a difference in how people respond to you.

(pages 85–86)

ON THE WATCHTOWER

For this section, you and your spouse need to work together in a semiprivate spot in the room to answer the following questions:

9. Return to your chart in question 3 above. Write the relationships in the left column, but this time discuss what you need to do together to keep those relationships from having a negative effect on your marriage. In other words, how will you guard your hearts?

The Relationship

What we will do to help but still guard our hearts and our marriage

_____ _____

_____ _____

_____ _____

PREPARE FOR THE WEEK

This week we are going to consider another relational enemy that poses a threat to our marriages, probably one that would be considered the most common—sexual temptation. You will need to read chapter 6 of Guard Your Heart.

We advise you not to go into this lesson thinking, I'd never do that, *or* I'm a Christian. That kind of temptation won't happen to me. *Believe us when we tell you that it happens all the time. We can't begin to recount the number of Christians who found themselves blindsided by this one. Sometimes they're able to get out before damage is done; sometimes they have to repent and rebuild; sometimes they run away and leave untold damage in their wake.*

Even if you think it won't happen to you, let's protect the castle anyway. You never know when the enemy might be planning a surprise attack!

Close in prayer.

Week Four—Day One

MY PERSONAL REFLECTION:
REMAINING FAITHFUL

During the week, you and your spouse should read chapter 6 in *Guard Your Heart*. The questions below will focus on some of the scenarios in the book. This chapter focuses on the problem of sexual temptation.

This week you and your spouse will wrestle with an enemy of your heart that can be so subtle that by the time you discover its presence, your marriage could be in serious trouble. Even if you would never consider committing adultery, you can still be vulnerable.

Read pages 87–90 and the scenarios Gary and Barb give of various situations.

1. In the first scenario, if Pam came to you and told you about her encounter with an old flame, what advice would you give her?

    _____

    _____

    _____

2. *Women:* If you were in Pam's shoes, what would you do to guard your heart? *Men:* If you were in her husband's place and you sensed a problem, what would you do to help guard your marriage?

    _____

    _____

    _____

3. In the second scenario, what has Sherry done to let down her guard?

    _____

_____

_____

4. What should Sherry do in order to guard her heart and her marriage?

_____

_____

_____

5. In the third scenario, what do you think might have happened to cause Roger to act as he did? Where did he let down his guard?

_____

_____

_____

6. In the fourth scenario, how did Stan get on the "runaway freight train"?

_____

_____

_____

7. At what stop should Stan have gotten off the train?

_____

_____

_____

Spend some time quietly in prayer. You may have never run into this kind of situation or have been tempted away from your spouse by another person. Thank the Lord for that, and ask him to continue to give you strength and wisdom in your relationships.

Perhaps today you know you are in the middle of a difficult temptation. You need to be brutally honest with yourself: to act on the temptation would be sin—no matter how good it might feel, no matter how much you think you deserve it, no matter how difficult it would be to cut off the relationship. Ask God to convict you, to show you what you need to do, and to give you the strength to do it.

Perhaps today you are simply toying in your mind with the possibility of a better relationship outside of your marriage. Turn away from it today. Ask God to give you the strength to do the right thing.

Finally, ask God to overwhelm you with love for your spouse. Tell God you want to do the right thing and rejoice in your marriage. Remember, love is not a feeling (although it certainly can be much of the time); love is a choice. You must choose to love today, whether you feel like it or not. That's the way to guard your heart.

Week Four—Day Two

COUPLE INTERACTION: REMAINING FAITHFUL

You will need to set aside about thirty minutes to complete this exercise with your spouse. Be sure you have selected a place where you will not be interrupted (turn off the phones, pagers, and find a location that will allow you to comfortably share with each other).

Begin your time together in prayer. As each of you prays, focus on the following:

- That you will be able to guard your hearts and be accountable to each other.
- That if there are breaches in the wall of your marriage, you will each seek to repair your part of the wall and protect your marriage.
- That you will be open to what your spouse shares with you.
- That God will be glorified by your marriage.

1. During your Personal Reflection time discuss the answers you gave to the questions about the scenarios in the book.

2. Talk about your own situation. Be willing to discuss your own personal fears or worries. Talk about how you can protect yourselves and each other in those situations. Discuss plans of action as needed.

Conclude your time in prayer. Ask God to give each of you the strength to do what is right, to protect your marriage, and to strengthen your relationship with each other.

Week Four—Day Three

MY ASSIGNMENT:
REMAINING FAITHFUL

You have two assignments this week:

1. Read chapter 6 of *Guard Your Heart*. Have you completed that assignment yet?

    ❏ Yes   ❏ No   ❏ I've started, but I have more to read.

2. Focus on being accountable to each other. Act to relieve any fears or worries your spouse addressed during your Couple Interaction time.

My Journal

How did your Couple Interaction time go? Were there any insights or breakthroughs? Explain.

_____

_____

_____

_____

_____

_____

_____

_____

_____

Here is what I did to guard my heart against temptation and to relieve my spouse's fears.

_____

_____

_____

_____

_____

_____

_____

_____

_____

Group Session Five

GUARDING AGAINST IMPROPER RELATIONSHIPS

OPEN THE DRAWBRIDGE

During the week, you and your spouse should have read chapter 6 of *Guard Your Heart*. Ideally you also made time to work through the homework assignments.

As the session begins, couples should work together to answer the following questions:

1. Perhaps it shouldn't surprise us, but Hollywood does a great job at making extra-marital affairs seem good and right and so well deserved by the actors in the stories. Describe one or two movie plots that glorified people having an affair as "the right thing to do."

    _____

    _____

    _____

2. Now describe a couple of movies that actually did show the power of marriage vows and how people stuck it out even through difficulty (there *are* a few movies that have done that).

    _____

    _____

    _____

How many times has the story as it unfolded on the screen been so intense that we found ourselves rooting for the marriage to end and the "in love" couple to be able to run off together into the sunset to live happily ever after?

Make no mistake about it, no matter who you are, no matter what kind of spiritual leadership position you may hold, no matter how strong you think your marriage is, your marriage castle needs to be protected from sexual temptation. Like the castles of old, a few years of neglect caused walls to crumble. Likewise, neglect of your marriage can cause someone else to step in with sexual temptation that you never thought could happen. Let's examine some of these situations today and explore what we can do to guard our hearts and our castles against improper relationships.

STAND GUARD

We discussed the difficulty of relationships in the previous lesson, but the same principles apply here. Fill in the chart below again, with your leader giving you the words if you don't remember them.

A legitimate relationship has become improper when . . .

I _____ my emotional, physical, and spiritual energy to the point that my _____ suffers.

I depend on this relationship to _____ _____ my spouse should meet.

I refuse to _____ to my spouse's concerns about this relationship.

I am not willing to ask my spouse for _____ with this relationship.

Gary and Barb say:
One of the most subtle and potentially destructive threats to your marriage comes in the form of sexual temptation. We use the word subtle *because it is rare to hear of someone being overtly and purposely seduced by a person other than his or her spouse. The enemy of your heart and home doesn't really need a gaping opening like that to ignite temptation. All he needs is a moment of unguarded fascination or attraction, a few unbridled thoughts about* what if? *Like a cancer, small impure thoughts can grow into a disease that will threaten the life of your marriage relationship.*
(page 91)

The Rosbergs point out that men and women are often drawn into marital infidelity in different ways. Because men are more visually stimulated, it is often physical attraction that draws their attention. For women, emotional attachment tends to be the strong pull. If another man shows more attention or kindness to her than her husband, she may be tempted away.

For the next exercise divide into two separate groups: men in one, women in another. In your groups, answer the questions below:

3. In what ways do you think you (as men or as women) are vulnerable to sexual temptation?

    _____

    _____

    _____

4. If you were to get involved in an extramarital affair today, what would be the repercussions in your home, your extended family, your job, your church, your friendships, your relationship with Jesus Christ?

    _____

    _____

    _____

5. How would you advise one another (in your group) to guard your hearts against sexual temptation?

    _____

    _____

    _____

Now, still in your small groups, discuss the "Guardrails to Faithfulness" that the Rosbergs suggest in their book (pages 98–103).

Four Guardrails to Faithfulness

Guardrail #1: A Strong Relationship with the Father

6. Why do you think this is important in order to guard your heart against sexual temptation?

    _____

    _____

_____

_____

Guardrail #2: A Cautious Relationship with the Opposite Sex

7. Where do you think we (as men or as women) should draw boundary lines in
   how we deal with members of the opposite sex?

   _____

   _____

   _____

8. Describe the importance of each of the suggestions below:
   Dismiss and replace tempting thoughts.

   _____

   _____

   _____

   Don't gaze too long; watch your eye contact.

   _____

   _____

   _____

   Don't go out of your way to meet someone.

   _____

   _____

   _____

   Be careful with physical touch.

   _____

   _____

   _____

   Keep conversation general.

   _____

   _____

   _____

When all else fails, RUN!

_____

_____

_____

Guardrail #3: An Open Relationship with Other Christians

9. In what ways can accountability with other Christians (of the same sex) help to guard your marriages?

_____

_____

_____

Guardrail #4: A Fulfilling Relationship with Your Spouse

10. In what ways can you (as men or as women) help to provide this kind of relationship with your spouses?

_____

_____

_____

ON THE WATCHTOWER

For this section, the small groups should now break apart into couples.

You and your spouse need to work together in a semiprivate spot in the room to answer the following questions:

11. Share some of the answers your groups gave for question 10 above. Then discuss what you each would like from each other in order to begin to build that kind of fulfilling relationship in your marriage.

    In order to build a fulfilling relationship with each other and so guard our hearts and our marriage against sexual temptation, we will

_____

_____

_____

PREPARE FOR THE WEEK

For the next two weeks, you are going to be looking at other enemies that could be potential threats to your marriage. We could categorize these last two threats under the descriptive title of "Extreme Lifestyles." You will need to read chapter 7 of Guard Your Heart, *which discusses the danger of an unfocused view of success and the cost that can be on your marriage.*

Close in prayer.

Week Five—Day One

MY PERSONAL REFLECTION:
DISCOVERING TRUE SUCCESS

During the week, you and your spouse should read chapter 7 in *Guard Your Heart*. This chapter discusses the threat that a misguided view of success can be to your marriage.

Consider the following questions and place a check mark next to your answers.

1. Is it okay to:

    Want to succeed? ❑ Yes ❑ No

    Desire to be the best you can be? To strive for excellence? ❑ Yes ❑ No

    Desire to serve and make the world a better place? ❑ Yes ❑ No

What is the correct answer to each question? Obviously, it is yes. However, the answer can quickly become no when we take any of these to their extreme. The following questions serve as illustrations.

2. Is it okay to:

    Want to succeed even if it means neglecting your spouse? ❑ Yes ❑ No

    Desire to be the best—to the point of obsession? ❑ Yes ❑ No

    Desire to serve and make the world a better place in order to feel important, earn awards, or feel significant? ❑ Yes ❑ No

What is the correct answer to each of these questions? Obviously, it is no, because each one of these attitudes is unfair and unwise. However, saying that you want to avoid these extreme attitudes is easy, but really avoiding them is very difficult.

This week, we are going to consider various attitudes regarding success. These attitudes reflect unhealthy extremes. They are

- a desire for success at any cost;
- a success drive that distances you from your spouse and children;
- an unhealthy view of success that leaves you feeling prideful, unsatisfied, or constantly envious of others.

These are enemies that attack your heart and will destroy those you love the most. The remainder of your reflection time will be devoted to considering if any of these attitudes is a problem for you. Take time to quietly and honestly evaluate your own heart.

Some of the "potholes on the road to success" that the Rosbergs have identified in chapter 7 are listed below. You have developed an unhealthy view of success if you are thinking that you will

- be a success only when you make your mark in the world;
- be a success only when you are financially secure;
- be a success only when you become the best at what you do;
- be a success only when you are somebody.

3. Write below what you most want out of life. How would you define success?

_____

_____

Understand that wanting a certain lifestyle, working toward a higher level of responsibility at work, wanting good things for your family, or setting goals in your life are not wrong in themselves. But along with your definition of success you noted above, you must also examine your motives. The Rosbergs identified several problematic attitudes toward success:

- Being willing to hurt others in your drive to succeed.
- Feeling prideful at where you are in life; looking down on others.
- Sensing constant dissatisfaction; no matter what you have, you want more.
- Worrying constantly that you won't reach your goal because of one small misstep.

4. Prayerfully consider the above attitudes, and ask the Lord if any of them is true for you. Be sure to listen, and be open to any change he might need to adjust in your heart and in your life. If you sense that God is pointing out some attitude that needs to be adjusted or changed, write that on the lines below.

    _____

    _____

    _____

5. Do you think your spouse would agree with your assessment? Why or why not?

    _____

    _____

    _____

Week Five—Day Two

COUPLE INTERACTION:
DISCOVERING TRUE SUCCESS

You will need to set aside about thirty minutes to complete this exercise with your spouse. Be sure you have selected a place where you will not be interrupted (turn off the phones, pagers, and find a location that will allow you to comfortably share with each other).

Begin your time together in prayer. As each of you prays, focus on the following:

- That you will share with an attitude of love for your spouse and commitment to the process of making any adjustments necessary in your life to defeat the enemies of your heart.
- That you will come to an understanding of each other's desires and views of success.
- That you will be open to what your spouse shares with you.
- That God will be glorified by your marriage.

1. Share with your spouse your responses from the Personal Reflection time.

2. Ask your spouse if he or she thinks your self-assessment is correct. Ask, "Do you think I've viewed myself correctly? Have I missed anything?" Write his or her response below.

_____

_____

_____

3. How can you help each other? As your spouse shares how you can help him or her, write these suggestions in the spaces below.

I can help my spouse defeat this enemy by:

_____

_____

_____

Conclude your time in prayer. Pray specifically that God will give your spouse the grace to defeat this enemy of the heart. Also ask God to enable you to help your spouse.

Week Five—Day Three

MY ASSIGNMENT:
DISCOVERING TRUE SUCCESS

You have two assignments this week:

1. Read chapter 7 of *Guard Your Heart*. Have you completed that assignment yet?

   ❏ Yes   ❏ No   ❏ I've started, but I have more to read.

2. Spend time this week seeking God's guidance. Consider what you thought about in your Personal Reflection time and what you and your spouse discussed in your Couple Interaction time. Ask God to search your heart and show you any kind of attitude that may be focusing on success at the expense of your spouse and/or family.

My Journal

How did your Couple Interaction time go? Were there any insights or breakthroughs? Explain.

_____

_____

_____

_____

_____

_____

_____

_____

_____

_____

Here is what I sensed the Lord saying to me this week about my attitude toward success.

_____

_____

_____

_____

_____

_____

_____

_____

Group Session Six

GUARDING AGAINST WRONG VIEWS OF SUCCESS

OPEN THE DRAWBRIDGE

During the week, you and your spouse should have read chapter 7 of *Guard Your Heart*. Ideally you also made time to work through the homework assignments.

As the session begins, couples should work together to answer the following questions:

1. What ways do you think people in your town view success? What is the standard people use to gauge others' success level?

   _____

   _____

   _____

2. What has been the greatest success in your marriage? Take a few minutes and record below one experience or achievement that you accomplished with your spouse, and explain why it was (is) so rewarding.

   _____

   _____

   _____

How do you define "success"? Too often it is unattainable—like having "enough" money. What is enough? When are you successful enough? When you earn a certain amount of money? What happens if you're earning that much money but still can't pay your bills or still aren't happy or still see someone ahead of you? What costs are you willing to pay to have the success you desire? What cost is your spouse having to pay for your drive for success?

Or perhaps you both have the same drive. You both are working long hours, hardly having time to spend a few moments together. You have goals, dreams, desires—but everything is out in the future. "Sometime when" are the first two words of many of your sentences. "Sometime when we have a bigger house, when we can afford to go on a nice vacation, when we have a certain amount of money in the bank, when we get that promotion, *then* we'll really live."

The problem is that no one knows what tomorrow holds. While you ought to plan, put away money for a rainy day, and set goals for the future, you also ought to realize that you need to enjoy *today*. You need to build your marriage today and every day. Don't wait to be happy "sometime when." Enjoy what you have today, even as you look toward the future.

STAND GUARD

3. Let's first consider the danger of the drive to succeed at all costs. As a group, read the following verses and answer the questions:

> Young man, it's wonderful to be young! Enjoy every minute of it. Do everything you want to do; take it all in. But remember that you must give an account to God for everything you do. (Ecclesiastes 11:9)

> Here is my final conclusion: Fear God and obey his commands, for this is the duty of every person. God will judge us for everything we do, including every secret thing, whether good or bad. (Ecclesiastes 12:13-14)

King Solomon was a great success by anyone standards. Wealthy and wise beyond measure, he presided over his country's Golden Age. Yet he also discovered that despite all he had, one thing was far more important—to fear God and obey his commands.

4. What does it mean to "fear" God? As a group, select each statement below that you feel accurately reflects what this means.

To fear God means that

❑ I respect him.
❑ I believe that he sees everything I do.
❑ I have an eternal perspective about everything I do.
❑ I will someday answer to him for all of my actions.
❑ I will do what he asks me to do.

5. Read the following verses, and on the lines below write what you learn from each verse about God's view of success.

> Potiphar noticed this and realized that the Lord was with Joseph, giving him success in everything he did. (Genesis 39:3)
>
> So the Lord was with him, and Hezekiah was successful in everything he did. (2 Kings 18:7)

_____

_____

_____

> From my experience, I know that fools who turn from God may be successful for the moment, but then comes sudden disaster. (Job 5:3)

_____

_____

_____

> It is not that we think we can do anything of lasting value by ourselves. Our only power and success come from God. (2 Corinthians 3:5)

_____

_____

_____

> We pray to God that you will not do anything wrong. We pray this, not to show that our ministry to you has been successful, but because we want you to do right even if we ourselves seem to have failed. (2 Corinthians 13:7)

_____

_____

_____

Tell those who are rich in this world not to be proud and not to trust in their money, which will soon be gone. But their trust should be in the living God, who richly gives us all we need for our enjoyment. (1 Timothy 6:17)

_____

_____

_____

6. Now, consider certain questions in light of these verses. As a group, answer these questions.

Is it okay to be successful in life? ❑ Yes ❑ No

Can you enjoy your success? ❑ Yes ❑ No

Does God care about your motives for wanting success? ❑ Yes ❑ No

Is being successful the most important thing you can do for God? ❑ Yes ❑ No

Therefore, your fear of God should guide you when you are pursuing success in any area of life. That is, when you stand before God to be judged for how you have lived, will God be pleased with what you have done to be a "success"? You need to consider if your achievement of success is going to cause you to sacrifice your relationship with your spouse. It is important to be absolutely sure that, like Joseph and Hezekiah, you are succeeding because God is with you and because you are being obedient to him in every area of your life.

Gary and Barb say:
On the surface, success and significance may seem like synonyms, but they really are not. For example, you can achieve great success in life—a six- or seven-figure income, perfectly obedient children, or similar accomplishments—without achieving meaning and significance. Ask Solomon. And you can enjoy a life of significance in terms of your relationship and service to God and others without achieving success by the world's definition. Furthermore, if you spend your life frantically trying to make your mark, secure financial independence, or attract fame, you may leave your family in the dust. But if you devote yourself to a life of spiritual and eternal significance, your quest by its very nature will include and nurture your spouse and children. Pursue significance, and you will guard your heart and home against the threat of the drive for success. Success is fleeting. Significance—our standing with God and everything we do in his name—lasts forever. (page 117)

ON THE WATCHTOWER

For this section, you and your spouse need to work together in a semiprivate spot in the room to answer the following questions.

7. During this lesson, you've considered several unhealthy attitudes toward success. But how do you avoid them? One way is to stop and ask some hard questions. Suggest some questions you could ask to help you avoid these destructive attitudes. Two questions are provided for you as examples.

    In our quest for success, we need to stop and ask ourselves:

    How is success different from significance?

    What is our real motive?

    Are we really trusting God with this?

    _____?
    _____?
    _____?
    _____?

PREPARE FOR THE WEEK

This coming week, you are going to be looking at another enemy that could be a potential threat to your marriage. This one focuses on issues of control and passivity. You will need to read chapter 8 of Guard Your Heart.

Admittedly, this may be a very difficult lesson. If you have these issues in your marriage, you may be tempted to skip this next lesson. However, that little warning signal may be telling you that this is exactly an enemy that you need to face.

In fact, your marriage may depend on it.

Close in prayer.

Week Six—Day One

MY PERSONAL REFLECTION:
SURRENDERING SYMPTOMS OF PASSIVITY OR CONTROL

During the week, you and your spouse should read chapter 8 in *Guard Your Heart*. This chapter discusses another threat to your marriage: the opposing problems of passivity and control.

Consider the following questions, and place a check mark next to your answers.

1. Is it okay to:

    Allow your spouse to make decisions in your marriage? ❑ Yes ❑ No

    Be a positive influence, and exercise leadership with either your kids or your spouse? ❑ Yes ❑ No

What is the correct answer to each question? Obviously, it is yes. However, the answer can quickly become no when we take these to their extreme. For example:

2. Is it okay to:

    Allow your spouse to make all of the decisions in your marriage? ❑ Yes ❑ No

    Be a positive influence by controlling your spouse to do what you want done? ❑ Yes ❑ No

What is the correct answer to each question? Obviously, it is no, because these attitudes are symptoms of either passivity or control—either one of which can be a poison in your marriage.

The quotations listed below are also on pages 123–124 in *Guard Your Heart*. Place a check mark next to any statements that sound close to something you have said (or close to how you feel) in your marriage.

SYMPTOMS OF PASSIVITY

❑ "It doesn't matter to me. You make the decision. I don't want to think about it."

❑ "Hey, I bring in the money. It's your job to raise the kids."

❑ "Hey, I raise the kids. It's your job to bring in the money."

❑ "If you want more romance and sex in our marriage, you have to initiate it."

❑ "I don't want to talk now. My favorite show is on."

❑ "I worked hard today. You go on to Katy's school program without me."

❑ "Family devotions was your idea, so you get to do it."

❑ "I don't care."

SYMPTOMS OF A TENDENCY TO CONTROL

❑ "I'll give you more money when I think you need more money."

❑ "We are going to my parents' for Christmas—period."

❑ *"I* make the decisions in this family."

❑ "It's your job to meet my needs."

❑ "I earn the money, so I decide where it goes."

❑ "I know what's best for the kids. We'll raise them my way."

❑ "If you don't get a better job, I'm leaving."

❑ "Do what I want, or there will be no romance tonight."

3. The statement that describes how I feel is:

_____

_____

_____

4. Looking at the statements above, I think . . .

❑ I have a tendency to be controlling.

❑ I have a tendency to be passive.

❑ I don't think that I have a tendency toward either extreme, but I could improve _____.

5. Spend a few minutes in prayer, talking to God about what you have discovered. Ask him to show you any symptoms toward passivity or control that you may not

be seeing. Be sure to listen, and be open to anything he might say that you have not yet considered. If you sense that he is telling you something, write it on the lines below.

_____

_____

_____

6. Do you think your spouse would agree with your assessment? Why or why not?

_____

_____

_____

Week Six—Day Two

COUPLE INTERACTION:
SURRENDERING SYMPTOMS OF PASSIVITY OR CONTROL

You will need to set aside about thirty minutes to complete this exercise with your spouse. Be sure you have selected a place where you will not be interrupted (turn off the phones, pagers, and find a location that will allow you to comfortably share with each other).

Begin your time together in prayer. As each of you prays, focus on the following:

● That you will share with an attitude of love for your spouse and a commitment to the process of making any adjustments necessary to defeat the enemies of your heart.
● That you will honestly discuss this difficult topic without hurtful words or condemnation.
● That you will be open to what your spouse shares with you.
● That God will be glorified by your marriage.

1. Share with your spouse your responses from the Personal Reflection time.

2. Regarding the issues of passivity or control, my spouse thinks that he or she:

   ❑ has a tendency to be controlling.

   ❑ has a tendency to be passive.

   ❑ Doesn't think that he or she has a tendency toward either extreme, but could improve _____.

3. Ask your spouse if he or she thinks your self-assessment is correct. Ask, "Do you think I've viewed myself correctly? Have I missed anything?" Write his or her response below.

_____

_____

_____

4. Discuss how can you help each other. Does one of you have a tendency to be passive because the other is controlling? In what ways can you bring your marriage back into balance in order to avoid these extremes? Write your suggestions below.

_____

_____

_____

Conclude your time in prayer.

Week Six—Day Three

MY ASSIGNMENT:
SURRENDERING SYMPTOMS OF PASSIVITY OR CONTROL

You have two assignments this week:

1. Read chapter 8 of *Guard Your Heart*. Have you completed that assignment yet?

   ❑ Yes   ❑ No   ❑ I've started, but I have more to read.

2. Spend time this week seeking God's guidance regarding symptoms of either passivity or control in your life. Consider what you thought about in your Personal Reflection time and what you and your spouse discussed in your Couple Interaction time. Ask God to search your heart and show you any kind of attitude that may be focusing on success at the expense of your spouse and/or family

My Journal

How did your Couple Interaction time go? Were there any insights or breakthroughs? Explain.

_____

_____

_____

_____

_____

_____

_____

_____

_____

Here is what I sensed the Lord saying to me this week about my attitudes of passivity or control in my marriage.

_____

_____

_____

_____

_____

_____

_____

_____

_____

_____

Group Session Seven

GUARDING AGAINST EXTREMES

OPEN THE DRAWBRIDGE

During the week, you and your spouse should have read chapter 8 of *Guard Your Heart*. Ideally you also made time to work through the homework assignments.

As the session begins, couples should work together to answer the following questions.

1. As you look back on your parents' marriages, would you say that they had issues of control and/or passivity? Explain.

   _____

   _____

   _____

2. Do you notice any of the same tendencies in your own marriage? Do you notice that you may be repeating a pattern because that is what you grew up with?

   _____

   _____

   _____

Sometimes we don't even realize something is a problem until we are challenged to look at how our marriages could be improved with a few changes. The issues of passivity and control can be very touchy to deal with because often the controllers can't see that their attitude is harmful and the passive members of the marriages are afraid to rock the boat! You might even feel as if your situation works for you, so you're tempted just to skip this chapter. We'd advise you to take a deep breath and be willing to tackle this issue. Your marriage can only get better because of it!

You may find that in your marriage, neither of you is at one of these extremes. But, as you noted in your homework, you can always find room for improvement in how you communicate and what you expect of each other.

The Rosbergs define *extreme passivity* as the attitude where one or both partners are lethargic in the relationship, tending not to take an active role at some point or in some areas. The passive spouse communicates through disinterest and inactivity.

The Rosbergs define *extreme control* as the attitude where the controlling spouse is not only involved but also tends to dominate to the point of excluding or devaluing his or her partner's involvement or contribution.

STAND GUARD

Let's consider the two-sided coin of the poison of passivity and the choke hold of control. As a group, read the following verses and answer the questions:

> As the Scriptures say, "A man leaves his father and mother and is joined to his wife, and the two are united into one." This is a great mystery, but it is an illustration of the way Christ and the church are one. So again I say, each man must love his wife as he loves himself, and the wife must respect her husband. (Ephesians 5:31-33)

3. The attitude we want to adopt is an unselfish love for our spouse. Whether you are a husband who is striving to be the leader of his home or a wife who is striving to respect her husband, you must have an unselfish love for each other. As a group, select all of the following statements that describe an unselfish love (check all that apply).

    If I am unselfish in my love for my spouse, I will . . .

    ❑ first seek to understand my spouse then seek to be understood.
    ❑ not demand my way.
    ❑ take the initiative to offer support.
    ❑ give up what I want for the benefit of my spouse.
    ❑ forgive my spouse for every offense.

4. Now, let's consider certain questions in light of what these verses are telling us. As a group, answer these questions.

Does God want me to view my spouse as an equal partner? ❑ Yes ❑ No

Does God want me to sacrifice my needs for the sake of my spouse?
❑ Yes ❑ No

Should I expect my spouse to agree with me all of the time? ❑ Yes ❑ No

Should I treat my spouse the way Christ treats me? ❑ Yes ❑ No

5. There are certain unhealthy attitudes that are common with the extreme lifestyle of passivity. Take the following survey to determine which of these attitudes is a problem for you. Answer each question based on how you might reply if asked on a scale of 1 to 5 (circle your reply).

Are you indifferent about making decisions with your spouse?

1	2	3	4	5
Not me!	*Maybe a little!*	*Sometimes!*	*Watch out!*	*Now you're meddling!*

Are you often angry with your spouse, but don't say anything?

1	2	3	4	5
Not me!	*Maybe a little!*	*Sometimes!*	*Watch out!*	*Now you're meddling!*

Do you tend to be passive because your mother or father was passive?

1	2	3	4	5
Not me!	*Maybe a little!*	*Sometimes!*	*Watch out!*	*Now you're meddling!*

Are you often discouraged with your spouse?

1	2	3	4	5
Not me!	*Maybe a little!*	*Sometimes!*	*Watch out!*	*Now you're meddling!*

Are you passive because you're trying not to be too controlling?

1	2	3	4	5
Not me!	*Maybe a little!*	*Sometimes!*	*Watch out!*	*Now you're meddling!*

6. As a group, suggest some advice for a person who struggles with passivity.

_____

_____

_____

7. Certain unhealthy attitudes are common with the extreme lifestyle of control. Take the following survey to determine which of these attitudes is a problem for you. Answer each question based on how you might reply if asked on a scale of 1 to 5 (circle your reply).

Are you afraid of not being in control?

1	2	3	4	5
Not me!	*Maybe a little!*	*Sometimes!*	*Watch out!*	*Now you're meddling!*

Are you often angry with your spouse and spouting at him or her?

1	2	3	4	5
Not me!	*Maybe a little!*	*Sometimes!*	*Watch out!*	*Now you're meddling!*

Do you usually have the attitude that says "my way or the highway"?

1	2	3	4	5
Not me!	*Maybe a little!*	*Sometimes!*	*Watch out!*	*Now you're meddling!*

Do you tend to be controlling because your mother or father was controlling?

1	2	3	4	5
Not me!	*Maybe a little!*	*Sometimes!*	*Watch out!*	*Now you're meddling!*

Do you tend to be critical of everything your spouse does?

1	2	3	4	5
Not me!	*Maybe a little!*	*Sometimes!*	*Watch out!*	*Now you're meddling!*

8. As a group, suggest some advice for a person who struggles with being controlling.

_____

_____

_____

Gary and Barb say:

The two attitudes represented by these lists of statements [on pages 123 and 124 of the book] are among the most harmful threats to your marriage. The first is passivity, _where one or both partners are lethargic in the relationship, tending not to take an active role at some point or in some areas. The passive spouse communicates through disinterest and inactivity, "That's not my job" or "I don't want to be involved."_

The attitude represented by the second list is control—_the other end of the spectrum from passivity. The controlling spouse is not only involved, he or she tends to dominate to the point of excluding or devaluing his or her partner's involvement or contribution._

Do you see yourself drifting toward or camped at one of these two hurtful poles? Are you a passive, uninvolved spouse or parent? Do you control or dominate your family relationships? If you fail to guard your heart against these attitudes, your marriage and family will suffer.

(page 124)

ON THE WATCHTOWER

For this section, you and your spouse need to work together in a semiprivate spot in the room to answer the following questions:

9. Are either of these extremes a problem in our marriage? If so, which one?

_____

_____

_____

_____

10. Discuss how you can help each other deal with this extreme. To defeat this enemy, my spouse and I will . . .

_____

_____

_____

_____

PREPARE FOR THE WEEK

Over the last few weeks, you have considered the common enemies of your heart and of your marriage. While you can follow biblical principles to defeat these enemies, you also need to make sure your marriage is built on a solid foundation. This foundation consists of fundamental beliefs that you must share with your spouse. During this week, you will consider these fundamental beliefs.

You will need to read chapters 9 and 10 of Guard Your Heart, *and then chapter 11 if you are a wife or chapter 12 if you are a husband.*

You're almost there! You've been doing a great job!

Close in prayer.

Week Seven—Day One

MY PERSONAL REFLECTION: INSPECTING THE MARRIAGE FOUNDATION

During the week, you and your spouse should read chapters 9 and 10 of *Guard Your Heart*. Chapter 9 discusses the importance of building your marriage castle on a solid foundation. Chapter 10 offers suggestions for how we can guard our hearts. In addition, if you are a wife, you should read chapter 11 about guarding your husband's heart; if you are a husband, you should read chapter 12 about guarding your wife's heart. (Actually, we recommend that you both read chapters 11 and 12.)

1. How well do you *know* your spouse? Take the following survey:

    My spouse's spiritual gift is _____.
    My spouse's best friend is _____.
    My spouse's lifelong ambition is to _____.
    My spouse's favorite hobby is _____.
    One person my spouse admires is _____.
    My spouse's greatest disappointment is _____.

2. If you want to guard your spouse's heart, you must also understand him or her. How well do you understand your spouse? Take the following survey:

    What is your spouse's most urgent need at this time? Why?

    _____
    _____
    _____

What is the most difficult temptation your spouse faces?

_____

_____

_____

Three things my spouse needs from me are:

● _____

● _____

● _____

Please follow the instructions for husband or wife.

HUSBANDS:

Chapters 11 and 12 of *Guard Your Heart* give advice to husbands and wives about how they can guard each other's hearts. The first set of questions below are from the chapter your wife will read about how to guard your heart. Consider each tip, and rank how important each one is to you at this point in your life. You will use a scale of 1 to 5 (1 = not at all; 5 = extremely important to me).

3.   How important is it to you that your wife . . .

help you achieve your dreams?

| 1 | 2 | 3 | 4 | 5 |

be alert to controlling tendencies?

| 1 | 2 | 3 | 4 | 5 |

love you unconditionally?

| 1 | 2 | 3 | 4 | 5 |

respect how you are different from her?

| 1 | 2 | 3 | 4 | 5 |

encourage you to find Christian men to help you grow spiritually?

| 1 | 2 | 3 | 4 | 5 |

recognize how influential she is in your life?

| 1 | 2 | 3 | 4 | 5 |

be wholeheartedly committed to you?

| 1 | 2 | 3 | 4 | 5 |

4. The next set of questions are from the chapter you will read about how to guard your wife's heart. Chapter 12 describes seven keys to guarding her heart. Determine one specific way you can follow through on each one for your wife. Record what you will do below.

I will . . .
ask, listen, and connect by _____.
offer practical help by_____.
make time just for her by _____.
give her time for herself by_____.
love her unconditionally by_____.
demonstrate spiritual leadership by _____.
pray for and with her by _____.

WIVES:

Chapters 11 and 12 of *Guard Your Heart* give advice to husbands and wives about how they can guard each other's hearts. The first set of questions below are from the chapter your husband will read about how to guard your heart. Consider each key, and rank how important each one is to you at this point in your life. You will use a scale of 1 to 5 (1 = not at all; 5 = extremely important to me).

3. How important is it to you that your husband . . .

ask, listen, and connect with you?

| 1 | 2 | 3 | 4 | 5 |

offer you practical help?

| 1 | 2 | 3 | 4 | 5 |

make time just for you?

| 1 | 2 | 3 | 4 | 5 |

give you time for yourself?

1	2	3	4	5

love you unconditionally?

1	2	3	4	5

demonstrate spiritual leadership in your home?

1	2	3	4	5

pray for and with you?

1	2	3	4	5

4. The next questions are from the chapter you will read about how to guard your husband's heart. Chapter 11 describes tips to do that. Determine one specific way you can follow through on each one for your husband. Record what you will do below.

I will . . .
help him achieve his dreams by _____.
be alert to my controlling tendencies by _____.
love him unconditionally by _____.
respect his differences by _____.
encourage him to find Christian friends by_____.
recognize my influence in his life by _____.
be committed to him by _____.

Before your time together this week, find a rock that symbolizes your "rock solid" commitment to your spouse and to a strong foundation for your marriage.

Week Seven—Day Two

COUPLE INTERACTION: INSPECTING THE MARRIAGE FOUNDATION

You will need to set aside about thirty minutes to complete this exercise with your spouse. Be sure you have selected a place where you will not be interrupted (turn off the phones, pagers, and find a location that will allow you to comfortably share with each other).

1. Share with each other how you answered questions 1 and 2. See if your spouse agrees with your answers.

2. Talk about how you ranked the "tips" and the "keys" to guarding each other's heart. As your spouse shares, go back to his or her exercise, and circle his or her answer so you will not forget how important this is to your spouse. You may discover something new about your spouse. If so, discuss it and try to understand your spouse a little better.

3. Conclude your sharing by explaining what you are going to do specifically to help protect your spouse's heart. Tell your spouse how it makes you feel that he or she is willing to do these things to guard your heart.

4. Exchange your rocks. You should give the rock you have chosen to your spouse as you repeat the following words. Make this a prayer of commitment to God and each other.

I promise . . .

    to never give up on protecting your heart;

    to give God my unconditional obedience;

    to give you unconditional forgiveness;

Amen.

Week Seven—Day Three

MY ASSIGNMENT:
INSPECTING THE
MARRIAGE FOUNDATION

You have two assignments this week:

1. Read chapters 9 and 10 of *Guard Your Heart*, plus either chapter 11 or 12. Have you completed that assignment yet?

   ❏ Yes   ❏ No   ❏ I've started, but I have more to read.

2. During the week, review the answers both you and your spouse gave to the questions in the Personal Reflection time. Prayerfully consider your spouse's needs, and ask God to show you how you can guard your own heart and how you can help to guard your spouse's heart.

My Journal

How did your Couple Interaction time go? Were there any insights or breakthroughs? Explain.

_____

_____

_____

_____

_____

_____

_____

_____

_____

Here is what I did to guard my heart this week.

_____

_____

_____

_____

_____

_____

_____

_____

_____

Here is what I did to guard my spouse's heart this week.

_____

_____

_____

_____

_____

_____

_____

_____

_____

Group Session Eight

GUARDING OUR MARRIAGE CASTLE

OPEN THE DRAWBRIDGE

During the week, you and your spouse should have read chapters 9 and 10 of *Guard Your Heart,* as well as either chapter 11 or 12 (or both, which is our recommendation). Ideally you also made time to work through the homework assignments.

As the session begins, couples should work together to answer the following questions.

1. What do guards do? Think of security guards, crossing guards, or guards high atop the walls or in the turret of a castle. What is their job description? How important are they?

    _____

    _____

    _____

2. What if the guards don't do their jobs?

    _____

    _____

    _____

Let's inspect the foundation of your marriage castle. Walk around the walls. Look at the corners. Do you see cracks? Holes? Places that need strengthening? Sections that might even need to be torn down and rebuilt? What building materials will you need? Gary and Barb suggest some "rocks" that you will want to build into your marriage foundation. Let's explore these today. After this study, you will want your marriage to be "on the rocks," for that phrase will have a whole new meaning!

STAND GUARD

The Rock of the Resurrection

The first "rock" you need in your foundation is the rock of Christ's death, burial, and triumphant resurrection. You see, without Christ's resurrection, there is no faith, no hope. We might as well "eat, drink, and be merry"! Why would we worry about serving our spouse or being faithful if it really doesn't matter in the end?

But it *does* matter. The Resurrection was a real event that gives meaning to everything we do. Read the following verses:

> All honor to the God and Father of our Lord Jesus Christ, for it is by his boundless mercy that God has given us the privilege of being born again. Now we live with a wonderful expectation because Jesus Christ rose again from the dead. For God has reserved a priceless inheritance for his children. It is kept in heaven for you, pure and undefiled, beyond the reach of change and decay. (1 Peter 1:3-4)

> For we died and were buried with Christ by baptism. And just as Christ was raised from the dead by the glorious power of the Father, now we also may live new lives. Since we have been united with him in his death, we will also be raised as he was. (Romans 6:4-5)

3. How does the "rock" of the hope of the Resurrection make a difference in how believers live? How is *your* life "new"?

_____

_____

_____

_____

4. How does the "rock" of the hope of the Resurrection provide a good foundation stone for marriage?

_____

_____

_____

The Rock of Your Salvation

The second "rock" you need is the rock of your salvation.

> But God is so rich in mercy, and he loved us so very much, that even while we were dead because of our sins, he gave us life when he raised Christ from the dead. (It is only by God's special favor that you have been saved!) For he raised us from the dead along with Christ, and we are seated with him in the heavenly realms—all because we are one with Christ Jesus. And so God can always point to us as examples of the incredible wealth of his favor and kindness toward us, as shown in all he has done for us through Christ Jesus. God saved you by his special favor when you believed. And you can't take credit for this; it is a gift from God. Salvation is not a reward for the good things we have done, so none of us can boast about it. For we are God's masterpiece. He has created us anew in Christ Jesus, so that we can do the good things he planned for us long ago. (Ephesians 2:4-10)

5. These verses teach that our sin is erased because of Christ's death and resurrection. But what does this mean? Based on these verses, complete the following statements as a group as your leader gives them to you:

   ● God forgives my sin and gives me new life because he is so rich in _____, and he loves me _____.
   ● Even though I was spiritually _____ because of my sin, he gives me _____.
   ● His forgiveness proves the incredible wealth of his _____ and _____ toward me.
   ● I cannot take _____ for my salvation because I don't deserve it.
   ● Salvation is not a _____ for the good things I have done.

6. What does the "rock" of your salvation mean to you? How has it made a difference in your life?

   _____
   _____
   _____

7. How does the "rock" of salvation provide a good foundation stone for marriage?

   _____
   _____
   _____

The Rock of Obedience to God's Word

The third "rock" you need is the rock of daily obedience to God's Word.

> Anyone who listens to my teaching and obeys me is wise, like a person who builds a house on solid rock. Though the rain comes in torrents and the floodwaters rise and the winds beat against that house, it won't collapse, because it is built on rock. But anyone who hears my teaching and ignores it is foolish, like a person who builds a house on sand. When the rains and floods come and the winds beat against that house, it will fall with a mighty crash. (Matthew 7:24-27)
>
> Those who obey my commandments are the ones who love me. And because they love me, my Father will love them, and I will love them. And I will reveal myself to each one of them. (John 14:21)

8. How does the "rock" of daily obedience to God's Word make a difference in how you live your life?

_____

_____

_____

9. In what ways does God's Word provide a foundation?

_____

_____

_____

10. How can the "rock" of obedience strengthen the foundation of marriage?

_____

_____

_____

Gary and Barb say:

Take a long, hard look at the present condition of your marriage's foundation. You need all three elements we have discussed in this chapter: the rock of Christ's resurrection, the rock of your personal commitment to the risen Christ, and the rock of daily obedience to God's Word. You can't pick and choose; it's a package deal. If you want to guard your heart and home against the assault on your marriage and family, you need a complete foundation. . . .

A vital relationship with Jesus Christ and his Word must be your number one priority in life. Without Christ as the Rock of your salvation, you will be vulnerable to the enemy's attacks on you and your family. Jesus doesn't promise Christians that there will be no storms in their lives. He doesn't make you impervious to attack. Rather, with Christ as your Lord and his Word as your guide, you have every resource you need to withstand anything life throws at you and even come out stronger.

Barb and I challenge you to acknowledge that serving God individually and as a family is your most important purpose in life. This is the cornerstone for guarding your heart and home. Nothing is more important. Yet nothing promises such extravagant rewards for you as a spouse and parent.

(pages 150–151)

ON THE WATCHTOWER

For this section, you and your spouse need to work together in a semiprivate spot in the room to answer the following questions.

In chapter 10 Gary and Barb discuss ways for spouses to guard their own hearts in order to protect their marriage. They give five principles for defending marriage and family. Each of the five principles is listed below. On the lines after each principle, write what you can do to take action in that area. After you each have written your answers, share them with each other. Write your spouse's response on the appropriate lines. You may not be able to act on all five of these right away, but write your answers as goals, things you will work toward doing.

PRINCIPLE #1: COMMIT TO THE TASK OF GUARDING YOUR HEART
To do this, I will _____
To do this, my spouse will _____

PRINCIPLE #2: ASK THE LORD TO PROTECT YOUR HEART
To do this, I will _____
To do this, my spouse will _____

PRINCIPLE #3: ESTABLISH OPENNESS WITH GOD
To do this, I will _____
To do this, my spouse will _____

PRINCIPLE #4: KEEP SHORT ACCOUNTS
To do this, I will _____
To do this, my spouse will _____

PRINCIPLE #5: BE ACCOUNTABLE TO OTHERS

To do this, I will _____

To do this, my spouse will _____

PREPARE FOR THE WEEK

You did it! You've worked for the last several weeks to learn what it means to guard your heart and protect your marriage. Remember the picture of your marriage as a castle. The next time you see a photograph of a castle in a travel magazine or brochure, cut it out and put it on your refrigerator as a daily reminder to guard your marriage castle.

Medieval castles always had guards. A king would not have thought of building his castle without the means and the men to protect it. Guards were stationed round the clock, always posted, always ready to sound the alarm should an enemy approach.

The castle meant a lot to the king. It was his home. It housed his family, perhaps many of his nobles, and most of his guards. A large enough castle might even house many of the knights in his army. It was worth protecting.

So is your castle, your marriage. It is valuable. It is your home. You must always be on guard, twenty-four hours a day, never slacking off. You must be ready to sound the alarm when it appears that enemies are coming toward the gates. You must be ready to close the drawbridge before it is too late.

To do this, you must guard your own heart. But because you and your spouse are a team, you should be ready to guard each other's hearts as well.

We pray that you will take the tools you have learned in this study to help you guard your hearts and divorce-proof your marriage!

Guarding Love

LEADER NOTES

We are so grateful for people like you, people who are willing to take on the responsibility of leadership! Your willingness to partner with us in strengthening America's marriages means that more and more families can be spared the ordeal of divorce. We are so excited about getting this message into as many marriages as possible across this country. We have called our campaign Divorce-Proofing America's Marriages, and the first book, *Divorce-Proof Your Marriage,* describes the six key kinds of love that every marriage needs in order to stay strong and healthy. One of those kinds of loves is guarding love, and that is the focus of our book *Guard Your Heart* and this companion workbook called *Guarding Love.*

We hope that you're taking on the leadership of your group to study guarding love because you're excited—you also want to spread this message to as many people as you can! You see, in order to make these sessions work, you, the leader, need to be enthusiastic about the topic. You're going to need to motivate the married couples in your group to read the book and do their homework assignments. The homework is not a requirement, but it is essential. Stress to the couples that they will get so much more out of this study if they are willing to *make* the time to do their assignments during the week. They won't take long, but the value of what they will learn—about themselves and about each other—will last a lifetime!

While you can work your way through each chapter along with the group without much extra assistance, these Leader Notes will provide some transition statements and instructions that may help.

1. Order and distribute the following books to the couples before the first session:

    ● One copy of the book *Guard Your Heart* for **every couple** attending.
    ● One *Guarding Love* workbook for **every person** attending.

2. Contact all attendees a few days before the first session to remind them of the time and meeting location. Ask them to arrive at least ten minutes before the session starts. **Remind them to read part 1 (chapters 1 and 2) in** *Guard Your Heart* **before the first group session.**

3. You will lead each session by reading the workbook lesson in its entirety. The participants will follow along in their workbooks and complete the exercises as you instruct them. Use the additional comments in these Leader Notes as you have the time.

4. Scripture passages are provided at appropriate times in the workbook. All passages are from the New Living Translation published by Tyndale House Publishers. This will make it easier for everyone to follow along from the same translation. You can have someone in the group read these passages, or you can read them to the group.

5. Begin each session with prayer. This entire study assumes that God has brought this group together. Consider the following when you pray with the group:

   - We recognize that God brought every person to this study for a reason.
   - We are excited to discover new things about ourselves and our spouses.
   - We expect God to use his Holy Spirit to teach us how to better guard our hearts and our spouses' hearts.
   - We give God the glory for the ways he will make our marriages better as we submit to his plan for us.

6. Consider how to help with child care. Perhaps your church youth group can help with this.

7. Room preparation:

   - Provide name tags, and ask attendees to prepare the tags as they arrive.
   - Have a list of all attendees who signed up. Ask everyone to verify that his or her name is on the class sheet. Have someone at a table near the entrance to welcome each couple.
   - If you are charging each couple for the books and workbooks, have someone at the table to collect the money for the books that have been distributed.
   - Make sure you have adequate seating for everyone.

8. A note about the structure of this eight-week study: Before the first session, your

group members should read the first two chapters in *Guard Your Heart* as those chapters form the basis of the discussion for Session 1. *Guard Your Heart* then spends the next six chapters describing six threats to marriages. Each threat will be studied at each of the next six group sessions. In each session you will be going over in depth what the couples read in their books and worked on during the week in their homework assignments. The titles for the sections are drawn from the analogy that a marriage is like a castle that needs to be protected. The outline for each session is as follows:

- *Open the Drawbridge* (couples work together on questions that will help prepare them for the discussion)
- *Stand Guard* (more in-depth review of material from the book)
- *On the Watchtower* (couples work together on application to their marriages)
- *Prepare for the Week* (touch on the next topic and assignments)

9. The homework sessions are very important, and you should heartily encourage the couples to work on them. The assignments won't take much time, but couples will get so much more out of the study if they do the homework pages. In between each group session, you will see three days of homework during which each couple can consider the particular threat that will be discussed in the next group session. Not only will the homework assignments encourage communication with each other about these issues, but the couples will also come better prepared for the group sessions. The layout of these pages is described in the introduction. Make sure to go over this with your group during the first session.

10. Pray for your group members each week. Ask God to intervene with his Spirit to empower each couple to understand and meet each other's needs.

Leader Notes: Group Session One

CHRISTIAN MARRIAGES UNDER ATTACK

LESSON PURPOSE

To help couples be aware that their marriages are under attack and that their heart is the key to protecting their marriages. In this session, couples will

- examine the biblical warnings about protecting their hearts;
- affirm their commitment to guard their hearts against any threat;
- express their love for each other.

LESSON PLAN

Begin with prayer.

Open the Drawbridge
Read aloud the material in this section, and discuss questions 1 and 2. Explain the castle analogy, and discuss how that applies to guarding one's heart in marriage.

Stand Guard
Read aloud the verses, and fill in the blanks in question 3 as a group. The correct answers are below:

- My heart affects <u>everything</u> that I do.
- I really don't know how <u>bad</u> my heart can get.
- God examines my <u>motives</u>.
- If my heart is <u>pure</u>, I will understand God better.

- The most important thing that God wants me to do is to love him with <u>all</u> of my <u>heart</u>.

Transition:

"We can see from the Scriptures that our heart is the place where we really decide how we will live. This means that any threat to our marriage really is an attack on our heart. That is why God warns us to be careful how we live."

Work through question 4, and have the group check the appropriate answers. Discuss as needed. Then answer question 5, "God warns us to be careful because our hearts are <u>vulnerable</u>."

Ask someone to read aloud the quote from Gary and Barb.

On the Watchtower

Divide the group into couples, and have them find a semiprivate area in the room where they can quietly work together on the charts in question 6. They should individually fill out the first chart. Then they should discuss the numbers they gave to the charts and fill out what their spouses answered on the second chart.

Prepare for the Week

Bring the couples back together. Conclude your time by briefly reading through the overview describing the six marriage threats that will be covered over the next six weeks.

Read the five ground rules. These are important in a group like this. Couples need to be encouraged to be positive, not to ever speak negatively about each other in front of the group, and to hold in confidence any sharing that occurs in the room.

Finally, explain the importance of the homework assignments. If you have time, read through the Introduction (pages xi—xii), which describes how the homework assignments are laid out. Make sure the couples understand that the first day of homework is Personal Reflection, where they will work individually. The second day is Couple Interaction, where they will discuss together. The last day is simply a checkup to make sure they have completed the reading, have begun thinking about applying what they have learned, and had opportunity to journal their thoughts.

Remind them to read chapter 3 of *Guard Your Heart*.

Close with this quote from *Guard Your Heart*:

Gary and Barb say:

Just like the castles of old, your heart and the hearts of your spouse and children are vulnerable to a variety of dangers from without and within. Solomon exhorts us to shore up the castle of our hearts against the enemies of our relationship with Christ, with our spouse, and with our children. This is no time to cut corners, look for shortcuts, or scrimp on essentials. The castle lord who saved a few pieces of silver on low-budget defenses likely paid for his foolishness with his life. You dare not make the same mistake. Your heart is too valuable. It must be protected at all costs.

(page 32)

Leader Notes: Group Session Two

GUARDING THE BALANCE OF CAREER AND HOME

LESSON PURPOSE

To help spouses to commit to making changes in their lifestyle that will enable them to protect their hearts against the threat of having career and home out of balance. In this session, couples will

- examine the biblical attitudes necessary to avoid lives that are out of balance;
- commit to making permanent changes in their marriage relationships;
- confess where they have hurt their spouses by allowing other things to become more important than their marriages.

LESSON PLAN

Begin with prayer.

Open the Drawbridge

Allow couples to work together on questions 1 and 2.

As a group, discuss question 1. Ask people to explain what they do to keep their schedules straight. Even have people show off their PalmPilots (or other PDA) or day planners if they happen to have them. Then read aloud the material in this section.

Stand Guard

Read aloud the material, and then work together through question 3. Talk about how the attitudes listed there could erode the foundation of a marriage.

Transition:

"Believe it or not, some people will question if all of these are truly symptoms of a life that is out of balance. Some people think that it is normal to receive more satisfaction at work than they do in their marriage. Other people feel that the acquisition of more possessions for their family justifies a career that forces them to spend more time away from their family. Unfortunately, such thinking is the result of the relentless attack of the enemies of the heart. Our society is no help, and our own nature, apart from the influence of Christ, willingly adopts the values of our society. During our session today we will examine the Bible to learn God's design for our work and what he expects of us."

Share answers to question 4 by reading the verses and considering what they say about what God expects our attitudes to be with regard to our work. Then discuss how those answers apply in marriage.

Ask someone to read aloud the quote from Gary and Barb.

Answer questions 5, 6, and 7.

On the Watchtower

Divide the group into couples, and have them work on question 8, individually first and then sharing their answers by following the instructions in this section.

Prepare for the Week

Bring the couples back together. Conclude this time by reminding them of the homework. Remind them to read chapter 4 of *Guard Your Heart*.

Leader Notes: Group Session Three

GUARDING AGAINST MATERIALISM

LESSON PURPOSE

To help spouses to commit to making changes in their lifestyle that will enable them to protect their hearts against the threat of materialism. In this session, couples will

- consider the difference between needs and wants;
- discuss the four P's that can change from being healthy desires to unhealthy obsessions;
- read the Bible to discover God's attitude toward materialism.

LESSON PLAN

Begin with prayer.

Open the Drawbridge
Allow couples to work together on questions 1 and 2.

As a group, discuss general answers to question 2. In other words, instead of having people share where they themselves may be struggling, ask, "What are some cultural symptoms that reveal how many people are caught up in materialism?"

Read aloud the material in the workbook.

Stand Guard
Fill in the chart as a group. On the left side are needs that we all have. On the right side, ask the group for suggestions for how that need could become a "want." (This is

not to say that wanting a top-of-the-line vehicle is wrong; the focus here is on understanding that sometimes what we want is not necessarily what we have to own in order to meet our legitimate need. This is especially true when we are reaching beyond our means in order to have what we want. We *can* stay within our means and meet our needs.)

Answer question 3.

Question 4 is another version of the consideration of needs vs. wants. On the surface, there is certainly nothing wrong with the desire for any of the four P's listed. But when they become someone's focus and obsession, they become severe problems in a marriage. Discuss with the group both the healthy and unhealthy desires for pleasure, power, possessions, and position.

Transition:

"The Bible has a lot to say about money, materialism, and contentment. However, it can be so easy for us to get caught up in the here and now—accumulating all that we can, striving to get to the top, seeking to have a certain status in society, and owning more stuff than anyone else. God wants us to be much happier than that. He wants to spare us the stress of worrying about these things by gaining an eternal perspective. While there is nothing wrong with having status or even stuff, it is wrong to be consumed with their pursuit. In other words, do you own the stuff, or does the stuff own you? Let's look at some Bible verses and talk about what God says about this issue."

Answer questions 5 through 9.

Read aloud the quote from Gary and Barb.

On the Watchtower

Divide the group into couples and have them work on questions 10 and 11.

Prepare for the Week

Bring the couples back together. Conclude this time by reminding them of the homework. Tell them to read chapter 5 of *Guard Your Heart*.

Leader Notes: Group Session Four

GUARDING AGAINST RELATIONAL PRESSURES

LESSON PURPOSE

To help couples guard against the pressures that the other relationships in their lives can put on their marriage. In this session, couples will

- examine the various relationships in their lives and the kind of pressures those relationships are putting on their marriages today;
- confess to each other when other relationships have prevented them from giving their best to their spouses;
- commit to help each other guard their marriages against relational pressures.

LESSON PLAN

Begin with prayer.

Open the Drawbridge

Allow couples to work together on questions 1 and 2. You could spend a few minutes having the group share their answers to both questions.

Read the introductory material aloud.

Stand Guard

Read aloud the paragraph, and then ask each person to place a check mark beside the relationships that are currently causing difficulty in his or her life. They should write the name of the person(s) in the chart at question 3 with a brief explanation. Each person should work on this individually.

Work together to fill in the blanks for question 4. The answers are below.

A legitimate relationship has become improper when . . .

>   I <u>deplete</u> my emotional, physical, and spiritual energy to the point that my <u>family</u> suffers.
>   I depend on this relationship to <u>meet</u> <u>needs</u> my spouse should meet.
>   I refuse to <u>listen</u> to my spouse's concerns about this relationship.
>   I am not willing to ask my spouse for <u>help</u> with this relationship.

Transition:
"Our discussion so far has been focused on examining the existing relationships that are causing stress in our marriages. Now, we want to consider what we can do improve our hearts' defenses so that these relationships do not pose a threat to our marriages. As is always the case, God's Word provides principles to give us some direction. These principles all lead to one particular attitude that we will need to encourage if we want to guard our hearts. There are three practical steps we can take. Let's look at these and the corresponding attitudes we need to encourage."

Now work on questions 5 through 8. The answers to each step are below. Allow the group to discuss how these steps and the Bible verses should be applied to their marriages.

>   STEP #1: Be <u>accountable</u> to your spouse.
>   STEP #2: Be <u>authentic</u> with your spouse.
>   STEP #3: Be <u>aware</u> of your spouse.

Read aloud the quote from *Guard Your Heart*.

On the Watchtower
Divide the group into couples, and have them complete question 9.

Prepare for the Week
Bring the couples back together. Conclude the session by describing this week's assignment. Remind them to read chapter 6 of *Guard Your Heart*.

Leader Notes: Group Session Five

GUARDING AGAINST IMPROPER RELATIONSHIPS

LESSON PURPOSE

To help couples strengthen their devotion to their spouses. In this session, couples will

- examine the subtle ways that legitimate relationships can become improper;
- examine the biblical attitudes necessary to guard against improper relationships;
- commit to staying within the "guardrails" that will protect them and guard their hearts.

LESSON PLAN

Begin with prayer.

Open the Drawbridge
Allow couples to work together on questions 1 and 2. Then spend a few minutes having the group share their answers to both questions.

Read the introductory material aloud.

Stand Guard
This same exercise was in the last session, but we have included it again because it applies not just to difficult relationships but also to improper relationships. Work together to fill in the blanks (see if anyone remembers the answers from last week).

The answers are repeated below.

A legitimate relationship has become improper when . . .

> I <u>deplete</u> my emotional, physical, and spiritual energy to the point that my <u>family</u> suffers.
> I depend on this relationship to <u>meet</u> <u>needs</u> my spouse should meet.
> I refuse to <u>listen</u> to my spouse's concerns about this relationship.
> I am not willing to ask my spouse for <u>help</u> with this relationship.

Read the quote from Gary and Barb.

Transition:
"Improper relationships happen in very subtle ways over time. Often people don't even realize they've fallen into the trap until it's almost too late. Many times people who think it could never happen to them find themselves drawn in. That's why it is so important for us to guard our hearts. We need to be constantly aware of ourselves, asking ourselves the difficult questions. 'Am I going out of my way to run across this person?' 'Am I letting myself get carried away with the attraction I feel for this person?' 'If I'm perfectly honest with myself, with what is going on in my heart and mind?' Far too often, no one thinks about the repercussions of his or her actions. It feels so good, it reignites a spark that may have gone cold a long time ago, it might even seem to be deserved. Let's divide into groups of men and women to discuss the questions in our workbooks."

Divide into two groups—one of men and one of women. Ask each group to answer questions 3 through 5.

Then the groups should continue on through the workbook, answering questions 6 through 10 under the heading "Four Guardrails to Faithfulness." Allow them plenty of time for discussion.

On the Watchtower
Divide the group into couples, and have them complete question 11.

Prepare for the Week
Bring the couples back together. Conclude the session by describing this week's assignments. Remind them to read chapter 7 of *Guard Your Heart*.

Leader Notes: Group Session Six

GUARDING AGAINST WRONG VIEWS OF SUCCESS

LESSON PURPOSE

To guide couples to learn how God's wisdom will help build a strong partnership in their marriage. In this session, couples will

- examine how well they work together in their marriages;
- determine if they have an unhealthy drive to succeed;
- commit to growing in wisdom together.

LESSON PLAN

Begin with prayer.

Open the Drawbridge
Give couples a few minutes to answer questions 1 and 2. Give some an opportunity to share their answers.

Read aloud the material in the workbook.

Stand Guard
Work your way through questions 3 through 5 by reading the Bible verses as a group and then answering the questions.

Transition:
"Now let's put all of these thoughts together. We've looked at many Bible verses that discuss what it means to be successful. This topic goes hand in hand with what we

discussed in Session 2 about keeping a balance in life and in Session 3 about material-ism (which often goes along with the trappings of success). It is important to realize that God often rewarded his faithful servants with great success. At other times, however, he called people to serve him, all the while telling them that they would fail (at least in the world's eyes). Obviously God's idea of success is very different from the world's. How do we apply God's view of success to our lives and to our mar-riages?"

Discuss answers to question 6. The answers to the first three should be yes; the answer to the last one should be no.

Read the material in the workbook, and the quote from Gary and Barb.

On the Watchtower

Divide the group into couples, and have them find a semiprivate area in the room where they can quietly work together on question 7.

Prepare for the Week

Explain the assignments for this week. Remind the couples to do their homework pages and to read chapter 8 of *Guard Your Heart*.

Leader Notes: Group Session Seven

GUARDING AGAINST EXTREMES

LESSON PURPOSE

To guide couples to consider their interaction based on the topic of control or passivity. In this session, couples will

- learn about the two extremes of passivity and control;
- study what God's Word says about how husbands and wives should love each other;
- do some honest self-assessment.

LESSON PLAN

Begin with prayer.

Open the Drawbridge
Give couples a few minutes to answer questions 1 and 2. (Because this is very private material, do not ask them to share their discussion with the group.)

Read the material in the workbook.

Stand Guard
Work your way through questions 3 through 5 by reading the Bible verses as a group and then answering the questions. Allow for discussion as needed.

For question 6, ask each person to individually fill in his or her answers on the chart. These will be kept private; no one needs to share. If a person discovers that he or she consistently rates these questions with a 4 or 5, then that may be an indication of some passive tendencies. This is by no means a clinical diagnosis; this is just a way of thinking about how they are interacting in their marriages and may serve as a warning sign.

Before proceeding to question 7, read the definition of *passivity* from the Gary and Barb quote (which appears after question 9 in the workbook). The definition is included below:

> Passivity [is] where one or both partners are lethargic in the relationship, tending not to take an active role at some point or in some areas. The passive spouse communicates through disinterest and inactivity, "That's not my job" or "I don't want to be involved." (page 124)

Ask the group to discuss question 7.

For question 8, ask each person to individually fill in his or her answers on the chart. These also will be kept private; no one needs to share. If a person discovers that he or she consistently rates these questions with a 4 or 5, then that may be an indication of some controlling tendencies.

Before proceeding to question 9, read the definition of *control* from the Gary and Barb quote (appearing after question 9 in the workbook). The definition is included below:

> Control [is] the other end of the spectrum from passivity. The controlling spouse is not only involved; he or she tends to dominate to the point of excluding or devaluing his or her partner's involvement or contribution. (page 124)

Ask the group to discuss question 9.

Read the Gary and Barb quote.

On the Watchtower
Divide the group into couples, and have them find a semiprivate area in the room where they can quietly work together on questions 10 and 11.

Prepare for the Week

Explain the assignments for this week. This week the couples have a little more reading to do. They should read chapters 9 and 10 of *Guard Your Heart*. In addition, wives should read chapter 11; husbands should read chapter 12. Of course, they can read both chapters 11 and 12 if they have the time. In fact, recommend it to them.

Leader Notes: Group Session Eight

GUARDING OUR MARRIAGE CASTLE

LESSON PURPOSE

To help couples discover how to strengthen the foundation of their marriage. In this session, couples will

- examine the importance of the truth of their faith in light of their marriages;
- examine the importance of their own personal relationship with Christ in the light of their marriages;
- examine the importance of their obedience to God's Word in light of their marriages.

LESSON PLAN

Begin with prayer.

Open the Drawbridge
Give the couples a few minutes to work together on questions 1 and 2. Have them share their answers with the group.

Read the material in the workbook.

Stand Guard
Read through the section called "The Rock of the Resurrection." Read the material, have someone read the Bible passage, and then answer questions 3 and 4.

Next, read through the section called "The Rock of Your Salvation." Have someone read the Bible passage, and then work together on question 5. The answers to the blanks are below:

- God forgives my sin and gives me new life because he is so rich in <u>mercy,</u> and he loves me <u>completely.</u>
- Even though I was spiritually <u>dead</u> because of my sin, he gives me <u>life</u>.
- His forgiveness proves the incredible wealth of his <u>favor</u> and <u>kindness</u> toward me.
- I cannot take <u>credit</u> for my salvation because I don't deserve it.
- Salvation is not a <u>reward</u> for the good things I have done.

Work together on questions 6 and 7.

Next, read through the section called "The Rock of Obedience to God's Word." Have someone read the Bible verses, and then work together on questions 8 through 10.

Read the quote from Gary and Barb.

On the Watchtower
Divide the group into couples and give them time to discuss this section. If they need help with some ideas to fill in these blanks, refer them to pages 157–164 in *Guard Your Heart*.

In Closing
Read aloud the Prepare for the Week section at the end of this session. Encourage the couples to continue to work on guarding their hearts. Thank them for coming, for their hard work, and most of all, for their commitment to their marriages.

APPENDIX

CAMPAIGN RESOURCES FOR DIVORCE-PROOFING AMERICA'S MARRIAGES

Dear friends,

The resources for the Divorce-Proofing America's Marriages campaign are designed *for you*—to help you divorce-proof your marriage. You and your spouse can certainly read and study these books as a couple. But it's only when you meet with a small group that is committed to divorce-proofing their marriages as well that you'll fully experience the power of these ideas. There's power when believers unite in a common cause. There's power when men and women keep each other accountable. To take on this challenge, you must have a group of friends who are encouraging you every step of the way.

There are several ways you can connect to a small group:

- Start your own Divorce-Proofing America's Marriages small group in your church or neighborhood. For workbooks, leader's guides, videos, and other resources for your small group, call 888-ROSBERG (888-767-2374) or visit our Web site at **www.divorceproof.com**.

- Give this information to your pastor or elders at your local church. They may want to host a Divorce-Proofing America's Marriages small group in your church.

- Call America's Family Coaches at 888-ROSBERG (888-767-2374), or e-mail us at afc@afclive.com and we will connect you with people and churches who are interested in Divorce-Proofing America's Marriages.

Yes, together we can launch a nationwide campaign and see countless homes transformed into covenant homes. But beware. If we do not teach these principles to our own children, we risk missing the greatest opportunity of all: to pass our legacy of godly homes to the next generation. Barb and I believe that, *for the sake of the next generation,* there is no more worthy cause. This holy fire must purify our own homes first.

Gary and Barb Rosberg

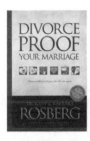 

DIVORCE-PROOF YOUR MARRIAGE
ISBN 0-8423-4995-2
Audio CD (3 CDs) ISBN 0-8423-6592-3
Audiocassette (2 cassettes) ISBN 0-8423-6894-9

**DISCOVER THE LOVE OF YOUR LIFE ALL OVER AGAIN
(workbook)**
ISBN 0-8423-7342-X

Your house is weatherproofed. But is your marriage divorce-proofed? In this foundational book of the Divorce-Proofing America's Marriages campaign, Gary and Barb show couples how to keep their marriages safe from the threat of divorce. Divorce doesn't happen suddenly. Over months and years couples can slide from the dream to disappointment and eventually to emotional divorce. However, they can stop the slide by learning to love in six unique ways. Small groups will enjoy the *Discover the Love of Your Life All Over Again* workbook, which includes eight sessions. Together couples will practice healing hurt in their marriages, meeting their spouses' needs, strengthening each other through difficult times, guarding their marriage against threats, celebrating their spouses, and renewing their love for each other day after day. A weekly devotion and assignment will help couples practice what they learn in the context of the encouragement of couples who are committed to the same goal of divorce-proofing their marriages. This workbook includes an easy-to-follow leader's guide.

THE 5 LOVE NEEDS OF MEN AND WOMEN
ISBN 0-8423-4239-7
Audiocassette (2 cassettes) ISBN 0-8423-3587-0

SERVING LOVE (workbook)
ISBN 0-8423-7343-8

You, too, can learn how to become your spouse's best friend with *The Five Love Needs of Men and Women* book and workbook. In this book, Gary talks to women about the deepest needs of their husbands, and Barb talks to men about the most intimate needs of their wives. You'll discover the deep yearnings of your spouse. And when you join a group studying the *Serving Love* workbook, you will learn how to understand and meet your spouse's needs within a circle of encouraging friends. They can help you find ways to meet those needs day after day, week after week. The workbook includes eight group sessions and three weekly activities. Easy-to-follow leader's guide included.

GUARD YOUR HEART
ISBN 0-8423-5732-7

GUARDING LOVE (WORKBOOK)
ISBN 0-8423-7344-6

We all need to guard our hearts and marriages. It's only in a couples small group, among like-minded friends, that you can get the solid support you need to withstand attacks on your marriage. In *Guard Your Heart,* Gary and Barb Rosberg outline the unique dangers and temptations husbands and wives face. In the *Guarding Love* workbook, Gary and Barb Rosberg give you the tools to show your small group how to hold each other accountable to guarding their marriages—no matter what the cost.

Do you know of a marriage in your church or neighborhood that is vulnerable to attack? Start a small group for that couple with the *Guarding Love* workbook as a resource. Or invite that couple to a small group that is reading and applying this book and workbook. The workbook includes eight exciting group sessions and an easy-to-follow leader's guide.

HEALING THE HURT IN YOUR MARRIAGE:
BEYOND CONFLICT TO FORGIVENESS
ISBN 1-58997-104-3
Available Spring 2004

FORGIVING LOVE (WORKBOOK)
ISBN 0-8423-7491-4
Available Spring 2004

In *Healing the Hurt in Your Marriage: Beyond Conflict to Forgiveness,* Gary and Barbara Rosberg show you how to forgive past hurt in your marriage, close the loop on unresolved conflict, and restore an honest, whole relationship with your spouse. You probably know a dozen marriages that are deteriorating because one spouse is holding a grudge or because the husband and wife have never resolved their conflict, hurt, and anger. And most marriages have past hurts that are hindering the ongoing relationship. Gary and Barbara Rosberg show you how to break free of these past hurts and experience wholeness again. The most effective way to heal wounds is within the circle of encouraging believers who understand, know, and sympathize with you in the common struggles in marriage. The *Forgiving Love* workbook is perfect for small group members who can encourage each other to resolve conflict and start the healing process. Includes eight encouraging sessions and an easy-to-follow leader's guide.

RENEWING YOUR LOVE: Devotions for Couples
ISBN 0-8423-7346-2

Have the demands of everyday life pressed in on your marriage? Has your to-do list become more important than your relationship with your spouse? Is the TV the center of your home, or the love you and your spouse share? This devotional from America's Family Coaches, Gary and Barb Rosberg, will help you and your spouse focus on your marriage, your relationship, and the love of your life. Let Gary and Barb guide you through thirty days of renewal and recommitment to your marriage by reviewing forgiving love, serving love, persevering love, guarding love, celebrating love, and renewing love through the lens of Scripture, reflection, prayer, and application.

Look for a persevering love book in the future from Gary and Barbara Rosberg and Tyndale House Publishers. This book will help you weather the storms of life without losing the passion for your spouse.

Also watch for a celebrating love book from your favorite family coaches, Gary and Barb Rosberg. This book will give you creative ideas on how to keep the fire and passion alive in your marriage.

MORE RESOURCES FROM THE ROSBERGS

40 UNFORGETTABLE DATES WITH YOUR MATE
ISBN 0-8423-6106-5

When's the last time you and your spouse went on an unforgettable date? Saying "I do" certainly doesn't mean you're finished working at your marriage. Nobody ever put a tank of gas in a car and expected it to run for years. But lots of couples are running on emotional fumes of long-ago dates. Truth is, if you're not dating your spouse, your relationship is not growing. Bring the zing back into your marriage with *40 Unforgettable Dates with Your Mate,* a book that gives husbands and wives ideas on how they can meet the five love needs of their spouse. Wives, get the inside scoop on your husband. Men, discover what your wife finds irresistible. Gary and Barbara Rosberg show you how, step-by-step, in fun and creative dates.

CONNECTING WITH YOUR WIFE
ISBN 0-8423-6020-4

Want to understand your wife better? Barbara Rosberg talks directly to men about what makes women tick. She'll help you understand your wife's emotional wiring as she shows you how to communicate more effectively and connect sexually in a way that's more satisfying to your spouse. She also reveals the single best thing you can do for your marriage—and why it's so important.

*Begin to divorce-proof your home, your church,
and your community today*

Contact your local bookstore that sells
Christian books for all of the resources of
the Divorce-Proofing America's Marriages
campaign
or
call 888-ROSBERG (888-767-2374)
or
visit our Web site at
www.divorceproof.com.

ABOUT THE AUTHORS

Dr. Gary and Barbara Rosberg are America's Family Coaches—equipping and encouraging America's families to live and finish life well. Having been married for nearly thirty years, Gary and Barbara have a unique message for couples. The Rosbergs have committed the next decade of their ministry to divorce-proofing America's marriages. The cornerstone book in that campaign is *Divorce-Proof Your Marriage.* Other books the Rosbergs have written together include their best-selling *The Five Love Needs of Men and Women,* as well as *Guard Your Heart, Renewing Your Love: Devotions for Couples,* and *40 Unforgettable Dates with Your Mate.*

Together Gary and Barbara host a nationally syndicated, daily radio program, *America's Family Coaches . . . LIVE!* On this live call-in program heard in cities all across the country, they coach callers on many family-related issues. The Rosbergs also host a Saturday radio program on the award-winning secular WHO Radio.

Their flagship conference, "Discover the Love of Your Life All Over Again," is bringing the Divorce-Proofing America's Marriages Campaign to cities across America. They are on the national speaking teams for FamilyLife "Weekend to Remember" marriage conferences and FamilyLife "I Still Do" arena events for couples. Gary also has spoken to thousands of men at Promise Keepers stadium events annually since 1996 and to parents and adolescents at Focus on the Family "Life on the Edge Tour" events.

Gary, who earned his Ed.D. from Drake University, has been a marriage and family counselor for twenty years. He coaches CrossTrainers, a men's Bible study and accountability group of more than six hundred men.

Barbara, who earned a B.F.A. from Drake University, has written *Connecting with Your Wife* in addition to several other books with Gary. She also speaks to women, coaching and encouraging them by emphasizing their incredible value and worth.

The Rosbergs live outside Des Moines, Iowa, and are the parents of two adult daughters: Missy, a college student studying communications; and Sarah, who lives outside Des Moines with her husband, Scott, and their son, Mason.

For more information on the
Divorce-Proofing America's Marriages
campaign, contact:

America's Family Coaches
2540 105th Street, Suite 101
Des Moines, Iowa 50322
1-888-ROSBERG
www.divorceproof.com